FROM NATURAL TO SUPERNATURAL

Healing God's Way

Dear Pete e Emma!
Be blessed with all His goodness
e all He has in store for you
— a radical life of faith, His Presence
e all that comes with this!

love Ange

DR ANGELA WALKER

FROM NATURAL TO SUPERNATURAL: HEALING GOD'S WAY

© Dr Angela Walker 2014
First Edition

Unless stated otherwise, scripture quotations are taken from the Holy Bible New International Version (NIV) Bible. Copyright © 1973, 1978, 1984 by International Bible Society.

Key words: healing, deliverance, spiritual, roots, supernatural, kingdom, medicine, missionary

Editor: Jessica S. Hosman
Cover Design: Steve Stone
Graphic Design: Bethan Wilson

ISBN -13: 978-1502325662
ISBN-10: 1502325667

Printed in United Kingdom

CONTENTS

Acknowledgements

I would like to thank everyone who helped out on the medical team, especially the core team of workers and also the visitors and students.

A very big thank you to Jessica Hosman, for all your hard work and sacrifice of many hours while editing this book. Without such gifting, spiritual insight and sacrifice, this book wouldn't have been published.

A big thank you to my brother-in-law Steve Stone for designing the cover.

And a big thank you to Bethan Wilson for doing the graphic design.

Dedication

I dedicate this book to the Great Physician Jehovah–Rapha, 'I am the Lord who heals you' (Exodus 15:26), from whom we receive all spiritual knowledge, revelation, wisdom and discernment into sickness and disease.

Thank You Father, Son and Holy Spirit, for teaching and demonstrating with such love and power how to heal the sick, bind up the broken hearted and set the captives free!

Endorsements

Dr Angela Walker has been a part of our Iris Global family for years, and we have truly reaped the benefits of her abandonment for Christ. Leading a naturally supernatural lifestyle is who she is in the bush, at our base in Pemba, or travelling to the darkest places bringing the love of Jesus. With a converted truck as a mobile clinic, she ventures to many remote villages in Africa listening to Holy Spirit. As she practices kingdom medicine, her three goals for the poor are setting captives free, bringing the lost home, and healing the sick. I believe this book will teach you to care for the oppressed, using God's mindset and it will also enlarge your heart for the hurting everywhere.

Heidi G. Baker, PhD
Co-Founder and Director of Iris Global

I think of Dr Angela Walker as one of God's special SAS forces; she is brave and courageous and seemingly quite fearless. She's willing to go to where few others in our profession as Christian doctors have gone, and for many if not most of us not even willing to contemplate going.

She is not against western, scientific or evidence based medicine, it is just that she has discovered a new dimension in the spirit where God leads her very specifically and very directly to embrace His healing power in wonderful and exciting ways. This book will challenge your Christian worldview, it will shake and disturb a comfortable Christianity, but be prepared to be challenged shaken and disturbed. It may lead you into a whole new understanding and experience of God, His incredible love, grace and mercy toward mankind.

It may well, as it has done for me, create in the reader a hunger for more and more of God in their life.

Dr Martin Panter
MBBS, MRCS, DTM&H, DRCOG, FRACGP, FRSTM, FACTM.
Adjunct Senior Lecturer in Medicine, James Cook University, Queensland, Australia
Founder and Chairman of HART (Humanitarian Aid Relief Trust), Australia

Foreword

Angela Walker is not your average medic. Highly qualified, professionally, she has chosen to put her faith in to practice, as well as her professional skills, and left medical practice to serve and minister to those in some of the hardest parts of the world.

The stories she will tell you will encourage some; amaze others; and cause some readers to wonder. The principles she will reveal through her story have been found in the real, not the theoretical, world of Christian ministry and many will transfer into the everyday life of every believer who is open to the leading and intervention of the Holy Spirit; for some it will challenge and even unsettle.

But Angela is a woman of truth, who holds to a fully Biblical worldview, and her mission in this book is to turn you to seek God in your own situation, and examine afresh how faith is applied. She was a member of the church where I served as Senior Pastor and my experience is of a woman of prayer, a passion for people becoming whole, and a personal commitment to act in Jesus' name. If this book draws you to the same 'disciple's walk' then her purpose will have been fulfilled.

Wes Sutton
Director of Acorn Christian Healing Foundation (UK)

Introduction

Little did I know God was about to turn my whole medical career upside down when He called me to be a medical missionary in Africa. After eighteen months working as a paediatric lecturer in Uganda, I could see myself working again in another hospital in Africa, but this time it was going to be different. God was about to derail me from my familiar medical path and lead me on a path I had never been down before. I would be going along unchartered territory.

My mind recalled a picture that a friend had shared with me. He saw me wearing a nurse's outfit and in my hand was a book with a red cross on the front cover. The book looked medical, but in fact it wasn't. It was the Bible. The physician I was working for was Jesus and I was to follow Him and take His orders. He was going to lead me to the people He wanted me to treat and would reveal their problems and underlying diagnosis. He would then reveal the treatment the person needed to receive and as His 'nurse' I was to follow and obey Him! The picture resonated with my spirit and I knew it was from God. As I made the decision to follow and surrender my life to Him, He took me down a path where there was no going back. It was a one way ticket. This is the path I want to invite you to also venture down.

This path has been the best adventure so far in my life, with much deeper insight into sickness and disease. It has transformed my life as a doctor. I will never see sickness and disease through the same lens that I did before. It has opened my mind to believe there can be spiritual as well as emotional roots to sickness and disease. I have discovered that sin, curses and witchcraft can inflict sickness and disease on the body; but I have also seen the power that forgiveness can have on our physical, emotional and spiritual health.

A few years ago the Lord gave me a vision of a huge white ship with the initials H.M.S. This ship was 'His Majesty's Service'. It was no ordinary ship. The captain was Jesus and He chose who could work in the various sections on the ship. The first job a newcomer was assigned to do would be one of menial tasks like making tea and coffee for the crew, cleaning the deck and a willingness to serve in any way required. Then at the appointed time, when the captain chose, He would move each person to a new role which came with greater responsibility. I saw myself being shown around the ship and was then taken to a new room. This room was pure white and spotless throughout. There was no shred of dirt to be seen. I then realised that it was an operating room. On one side there were medical tools to do minor surgical operations such as lancing abscesses, cleaning and suturing wounds, removing foreign bodies or excising lesions. Then in the centre of the room was an operating table. I thought, 'What is this used for and who is in charge?' Then in walked the surgeon, Jesus Himself. He knew exactly what the problem was and what major operation the individual needed to undergo. I was there to simply assist Him, handing Him the tools as He requested. One of the operations Jesus performed was major open heart surgery. I watched in awe as people got up off the table healed and fully restored.

I believe this vision was a parallel between natural medicine and supernatural medicine. The ship represented ministry work and before you could enter the healing ministry you first had to be willing to serve others and have a humble heart. There was no place for pride on the ship. The minor operations were quick healings that the Lord had equipped us to do like breaking curses, receiving cleansing and forgiveness of sins, breaking the power of witchcraft, binding and casting out demons. However, the major operations Jesus did and we assisted Him by following His instructions. The results were the person was completely healed in body, soul and spirit.

I decided to write this book after being inspired and encouraged by the many who have worked alongside me on the mission field. For me, it has been a privilege to learn on the job from the Great Physician Himself as I chose to follow Him, leaving my familiar, secure path and choosing a road I didn't really want to go down. Yet in truth, this path has opened my eyes to see much clearer into sickness and disease.

This book is for those who have a passion to see the 'sick' healed and made whole, and for those hungry to discover different ways of doing Kingdom medicine. I pray, by the power of the Holy Spirit, that you will receive all wisdom, knowledge and spiritual insight into sickness and disease. As God has transformed my life on healing the sick, so may He transform yours!

Chapter 1

SURRENDERED LIFE

*'Whoever finds his life will lose it and whoever
loses his life for My sake will find it'.
(Mathew 10:38-39)*

It all started when I decided to take a two month sabbatical. I had just finished a locum consultant job in a London hospital, when I felt the stirring in my spirit to take time out. My two month sabbatical ended up being five months as I relished my time hanging out with God each day, both in reading His Word and in listening to His Spirit. I had no plans or agenda except to know Him more and let Him do whatever He wanted to in me. It became a significant turning point in my life.

At the end of the five months, I once again felt the desire to return to work as a paediatrician. However, I sensed in my inner being that things were going to be different. God was redirecting my path. Instead of returning to a full time job like before, I would be returning to do part time hospital work. The other part of my time was to be taken up studying at All Nations Christian College (ANCC), a mission training Bible college in Hertfordshire, England.

In the vast library at ANCC was a huge section on witchcraft. I tried to avoid this section for it was not my interest or field of work, but I felt the Holy Spirit prompt me to read some of the literature. Then one day as a lecturer was speaking about the different types of witchdoctors operating in the different nations, I heard in my mind God say, *'You are the good doctor I am sending to My people. They only know about the witchdoctor when seeking medical help, but you will point them to Me, their Great Physician'*. I had such a deep sense of peace that I no longer felt any concern about coming into contact with witchdoctors or those who had been involved in any witchcraft. My time at the Bible College was a stepping stone before venturing to Africa.

My Will or God's Will

After just one year at Bible College I felt the same stirring in my heart to do mission work in Africa as I once did when I was a teenager. *But where and with whom?*

In the meantime I was trying to work out what job I should look for in Africa. I had acquired over the years many qualifications, skills and experience which I didn't want to waste. I then came to the point where I felt challenged in my spirit to lay all my skills before God. So I then had a choice to make. I could either hold onto my skills and try and find a job where they could be of use, or I could lay them all down before God and simply follow Him. The Holy Spirit convicted me with what Oswald Chambers said: *'God can do nothing with the man who thinks he is of use to God! We should be not out for our own cause but the cause of God'*[(1)].

I believe that we are of no use to God when we come to Him with all of our skills and ideas, wanting to lead our own life doing what we want and hoping He will be in agreement with us. The truth is God wants us to *co-labour* with Him. That means doing things His way with the leading of His Spirit. But His first desire is for us to be loved by Him and know Him intimately, then co-labour with Him. He so wants to share His heart with us for His people and open doors to send us out to work for Him in the power of His Spirit.

A dear friend when praying had a picture of me dressed as a nurse carrying a white book with a red cross on it. I thought there was confusion for surely this wasn't me. Then he interpreted that, as a nurse, I was to follow the physician's orders. The physician was of course, Jesus. Jesus would lead me to the people He wanted me to go to, reveal their diagnosis or underlying problems and what treatment to give them. The book which looked like a medical book was actually the Bible. Though in the natural realm I may be a doctor, in the supernatural realm there is only one doctor, Jesus. Hence as His followers, we are more like His spiritual nurses. This was very humbling for me to receive.

The Cost of True Sacrifice

One Sunday at my church, I noticed a white box hanging on the wall. I would not normally look at this, but I felt the Holy Spirit was drawing my attention to it. There was a red cross on it and under it was written 'First Aid'. He then said to me, *'It is all about My cross. You will reach out to My people and give them first aid by choosing a life laid down for Me. And through My cross, you will bring them into My Kingdom and I will heal them'*. I saw my life was to have His cross at the centre of whatever I do. For the cross is centred on His love, forgiveness and healing power, but is also a call for us to lay down our lives for Him... that is if we really choose to follow Him.

As I entered into the worship, I became overwhelmed with the Presence of God. Tears streamed down my face and it was as if it was just Him and me in the room. The worship song was all about His cross and His dying love for us. I wept as the lyrics flowed:

See His love nailed onto a cross,
Perfect and blameless life,
Given as sacrifice
See Him there all in the Name of Love,
Broken yet glorious, all for the sake of us.

This is Jesus in His Glory,
King of Heaven dying for me
It is finished, He has done it,
Death is beaten, Heaven beckons me.

Greater love no one could ever show,
Mercy so underserved, Freedom I should not know,
All my sin, all of my hidden shame,
Died with Him on the cross,
Eternity won for us
Such love, such love is this for me.... [2]

11

Suddenly, I had a vision and saw Jesus on the cross. He seemed three times the size of a man and was looking down to me. He then said to me (in a non-audible voice), *'I have sacrificed My life for you. Will you sacrifice your life for Me?'* Everything in my life flashed through my mind - my medical profession, possessions, home, relationships and finances. *Was I willing to lay it all down for Him?* I knew it was time to truly let it all go! There was no going back or holding onto anything anymore. It was as if I had nothing but Him.

I finally said, *'Yes, I am willing'*. I saw the cost and it was huge. It was everything I had, everything that I was or that mattered to me. But this was the real price I had to pay to follow Jesus. This is what it means to follow Him to the cross and completely surrender ourselves and the right to our own lives. It costs us everything, just as it cost Jesus Himself *everything*!

Jesus had no home, no possessions, no job status or salary (except that of a carpenter's son). That which He owned, was just the clothes He wore. He had a mobile clinic, for He was on the move and healed all those who were brought to him with a touch or a word. He simply chose to do only that which pleased His Father and was according to His Father's will. He knew His reward was in Heaven and He invested in nothing in this world except the people whom the Father led Him to. He relied on His Father for everything. All His needs were met in His relationship with His Father.

Surrender Paediatrics

Some weeks later I was walking in my local forest, praising God and shouting aloud in my spirit, *'Lord, I surrender my life to You!'* This wasn't the first time I had said this, but this day was different. Within minutes I went from feeling an overwhelming joy in my spirit to feeling a deep sense of grief within. It felt like there had been a sudden death in my family and I was now in mourning. I asked God if there had been a death and what was going on. He answered, *'Yes, you are mourning a death. It is death to your paediatrics. You cannot be married to paediatrics and Me. It has to die so you can be married to Me'*.

What a shock this was! I had been married to my work all these years and was not even aware of it. I had lived and breathed paediatrics and God had come second to it without me being aware. How confused I felt, for I thought God had called me to paediatrics, especially for my work in Africa. I just cried and wept deeply within, since it had been such a big part of my life.

I sought advice from some of the elders and leaders in my church as to what was the meaning of it all. They encouraged me saying, '**Where there is a death, there is also a resurrection**' and '**for the joy set before Him, Jesus endured the cross**' (Hebrews 12:2). I had to have faith and trust God as to where He was taking me next and what He had in store for me. Though at the time I felt quite alone and didn't understand what He was doing, it was the path He had marked out for me and only I could walk down it. No one else could walk it for me. If God was putting to death my paediatrics then I knew He would resurrect it His way, whatever that was, and there would somehow be joy in this.

As we choose to die to our desires, securities, comforts and ambitions, then we can experience more of the Holy Spirit dwelling in us and we can step into the work God has commissioned us to do with Him. He can't release us fully into His Kingdom work without us fully surrendering our all to Him. We must not be confused with the fact that if we are doing 'good Christian work' or 'ministry' then surely this is what He desires for us. No, He desires for us first and foremost to be intimate with Him and our work to be an overflow of His Spirit dwelling in us. It is not about our agenda but rather asking, 'What is His agenda?'

Jesus only followed His Father's will, for He did each day only as He saw His Father doing. He said the Son can do nothing by Himself but only do as He sees the Father doing (John 5:19). Jesus regularly spent time alone with His Father, listening to Him and knowing His will before He stepped into His daily work (Mathew 14:23, Mark 1:35).

Jesus knew that His life was not His own, for He had surrendered it to His Father. Jeremiah also knew this, '*I know, O Lord, that a man's life is not his own, it is not for a man to direct his steps*' (Jeremiah 10:23).

The grieving of my paediatrics went on for a few months until it seemed like God was taking me into the next part of my journey with Him. God was preparing me to go with Him to the dark nations. This was confirmed one day when a good friend, who is normally tone deaf, sang in tune a song prophesying my call to dark nations. I knew she was under the anointing of the Holy Spirit (for I had never heard her sing in tune before!). I had never wanted to go to the dark nations, so I was not very happy when I heard this. But likewise, I knew God would do something in me if He wanted me to go.

I realised that the enemy will try and stop us from entering our calling and one of the weapons he uses is fear. To overcome my fear of going to dark and dangerous nations, God gave me something like a modern day proverb: '*It is safer to be with God in a dangerous place than it is to be alone in a safe place*'.

It doesn't matter how dangerous something may be, as long as we are in His will and He is with us. The safest place we can ever be is in the will of God! Though the dying process had been hard, I now saw myself with the Lion of Judah going into enemy territory but completely protected - for He was with me, or rather, I was with Him!

Chapter 2

MISSION SCHOOL MEDICINE

'The harvest is plentiful but the labourers are few.
Ask the Lord of the harvest to send out labourers
into His harvest field'.
(Luke 10:2)

Here I was, having finished my year at Mission Bible College with no clue as to what I would be doing or where I would be going next. I knocked on the doors of missionary organisations but all that seemed available were hospital jobs where you had to fit into a structured post. In my spirit I knew that rather than staying inside the hospital walls, God wanted me to go with Him into different communities, reaching out to those who are unable to get to the hospitals.

I had a vision when praying, of a yacht out at sea with its sail up. In the vision there was minimal breeze out at sea and though it seemed 'common sense' to pull the sail down, the Holy Spirit said, 'Leave it up and get ready, for a wind is about to come and you must catch it so it can blow your sail to your next destination'. If I pulled my sail down, I would miss the launch forward and just spin around in circles. I was to get ready for something to come where the Holy Spirit would blow me into my next destination. I knew that this was what it meant to 'wait on the Lord'. Waiting here is active and not passive. It is a sense of getting ready for what God is about to do next. There is a sort of tension, like the string of a bow being pulled back and waiting to be released, before then shooting the arrow forth.

During this time of waiting, a friend was praying and had an interesting picture of me walking past shop windows. There was a certain window that I seemed to brush by and casually dismiss. But, if I looked in more detail through this window, I would see a pearl in the room. This was the gem or gift that God wanted me to have next (Mathew 13:44-46). As I pondered on this it came to my mind that the windows were the different mission organisations I had been looking into. But there was actually one I had previously dismissed because I thought it was not for me. It was Iris Ministries, now known as Iris Global[1].

I had previously let my common sense and logical reasoning dismiss the thought of working with Iris Ministries. But now, after having laid down my paediatric career, it looked like I should revisit this possibility and take a much closer look through the window of Iris. As I found out more, there was a quickening in my spirit and I felt God was connecting me to this missionary organisation for what He had next in store. God had been stirring my heart to be a labourer for His harvest and also had been calling me to lay down my life for Him. He had even shifted my way of thinking from natural medical work to spiritual medical work.

God opened the door for me to join Iris Ministries in Africa, but first I had to attend their mission school. I didn't really know what would happen after that because God wasn't going to show me yet... but I would soon find out.

Holy Given Mission School
It was the third 'Holy Given Mission School' Iris Ministries had conducted. This was a two month school which centred on being holy and given unto God, with the option of going on a two week outreach at the end.

My first day as I arrived at the Iris base was challenging. It was going to be two months of community life, living out of a suitcase, sharing a room with three other women and having intermittent access to running water. There was little space for privacy and you had to seek God's Presence amidst the chaos and noise going on around you. In spite of this, it was exciting to meet people from all over the world and hearing their testimonies as to how God had led each one of them to the school. Some, like me, didn't know what they would be doing after the school.

16

Professionally, I was not on my own either for there were around seven other doctors and some nurses also attending the school. However, I felt that God wanted me to put down my medical tools and now focus on the spiritual side to health. Therefore, if anyone came to me for medical advice I was to do something different - to seek God first and pray for them.

Spiritual Roots to Symptoms

Early on, one member of staff approached me with a red, inflamed eye that would not get better with anti-inflammatory or antibiotic topical eye treatment. So I simply asked if I could pray. Whilst praying it came to my mind that God wanted to increase His spirit of discernment for this person and I was to pray against any spiritual opposition to this. Though there was no immediate healing, when I next saw the person, they said that their eye had fully healed by the next day.

Later, another staff member asked if I could do anything for her hearing for she kept hearing ringing noises and a buzzing sound in both ears. She had already seen an ENT (Ears, Nose and Throat) specialist in her own country, but they couldn't do anything to help her. We prayed and God showed me that He wanted to whisper His thoughts to her as she preached and taught on His Word so she would speak straight from the heart of God. It was the enemy who was blocking this with the ringing sounds she had. After coming against the ringing in the Name of Jesus, I prayed she would be able to hear the still, quiet voice of God each day. When I next saw her, she said the ringing had stopped, though she still had a minor buzz. These were interesting cases for as I prayed God showed me what was happening in the spiritual realm and that by dealing with the spiritual aspect then the physical was being dealt with too!

One young woman attending the school had been sick with diarrhoea and vomiting. When I initially saw her I was medically thinking of infective causes for her acute gastro-enteritis including malaria. But further questioning revealed that she 'poorly responded to medicines' and had taken many drugs with 'no response'. So she was told by other doctors that she probably had a 'poor immunity' and was 'resistant' to treatment.

17

Something didn't sound right to me. Then when further questioned if she had any enemies, she said she was on a hit list by a group of Satanists. This now made more sense. So, I got her housemates and others to surround her and we broke off the power of witchcraft and curses and spoke healing and life over her body. Major stuff happened in her that day and her symptoms got better. Spiritual breakthrough led to her physical healing. She was resistant to medical treatment simply because her illness wasn't infective in nature. She had a spirit of affliction which, when broken in the Name of Jesus, enabled her to be both free and healed, through the power of the Holy Spirit.

These were just some of the initial teachings where God revealed a spiritual root to the physical symptoms. I was a novice, yet intrigued to find out more.

Outreaches

Each mission student was given the opportunity to go on a weekend outreach. This was something new to me and not really my cup of tea, since I had never really liked camping and I didn't see myself as an evangelist. On each team, there was a mixture of African Bible school students along with international mission school students who would reach out in the rural villages with God's love and Kingdom power. During the weekend, we would show love to the local people, preach the Gospel and show a film about the life and ministry of Jesus in different tribal languages, followed by praying for the sick.

Going on an outreach and living in the 'bush' made the basic life back at the base seem luxury. I couldn't wait to have a shower and use a flush toilet on return. It was hard to wash when the only water you had was bottled drinking water. During this time, a nurse had a word for me that the work God had next would be one where I would get my hands dirty. This is something that you avoid doing in the medical profession yet God in His sense of humour was preparing me to do such work as this.

One of the things I learnt on this first outreach was not to focus on the disease and try dealing with the problem by myself, but to actually get to know the Holy Spirit more personally and do as He says or asks. I had been so used to solving people's problems by myself and asking God to help me when I needed Him, but now He wanted to be included from the start. I had to change my focus from myself being the answer to looking to God for the solution. *Do we want to be healers or followers?* We learn by following and doing as He does. That's what Jesus did as He did only what He saw His Father was doing.

Shifting Mindsets

The mission school was a time of being stretched in all directions. It felt uncomfortable in places but I knew God was doing a deeper work in me that would change me for the good.

For thirteen years or so as a western doctor I had developed my thinking on a scientific mindset but now was a time to develop it further into a Kingdom mindset. *What did this mean? Was I going to lose all my medical knowledge?* I had already laid down my paediatric career before I came to the mission school. Now I felt I was challenged to lay down all of my medical knowledge and experience. I had no idea what the outcome would be but it felt scary. *What if God removed my medical knowledge and insight from me? Was this going to happen?*

I can now say in hindsight that God was simply expanding what I already knew into a much larger sphere of medical practice. I was now being able to see from God's perspective, that is, a spiritual insight as well as medical insight into sickness and diseases. How we so need this in the medical and healing profession! It is common practice to focus on our physical bodies when dealing with symptoms yet fail to remember that our body is linked to our soul (mind, will and emotion) and spirit (inner being). It is how we were created and we can't deal with one by ignoring the other or putting them in separate boxes. It just doesn't work like that. I could give out medical drugs to patch up the symptoms, especially some of the chronic problems like chronic body aches, or I could try and look deeper into the problem and get to the real root so the problem is not only solved, but prevented from recurring.

Through my experience, I believe there are spiritual and emotional roots for many illnesses where scientific medicine has not yet been able to find a cure. To put it another way, the reason

19

there have been no cures for many chronic diseases is because the researchers are looking in the wrong direction.

Next Steps

It was getting to the end of the school and I was wondering what God had next. So I decided to take a long walk. God spoke to me through a little child whom I saw running, wearing rags and had nothing on her feet. She ran straight up to me with a beaming, beautiful smile and handed me a small object. I thanked her and she ran off. When I looked at the object, I saw it was a mixture of sand and grit. I then threw it down thinking nothing of it and wondering why she gave it me. Instantly, I was convicted by the Holy Spirit. *'Would you do this to My children?'* I was stunned to hear this. The Holy Spirit went on to say that each grain of sand represented one of His children. *Was I willing to reach out to them?* I was then drawn to read the verse, *'By faith, Abraham obeyed and went, even though he didn't know where he was going. By faith he made his home in the Promised Land like a stranger in a foreign country; he lived in tents...' (Hebrews 11:8).* This stirred my spirit, but unknown to me at the time, my future was going to involve living in tents! God simply kept from me the fact that I would be camping every time I went on a medical outreach.

As I pondered on these thoughts I was then invited to come along to a meeting concerning the potential of a future clinic at the base. After sharing my views that there was also the need for a mobile clinic, all eyes turned to me. Though I wasn't volunteering myself, I somehow felt challenged to take it on. God then spoke to my spirit that I was to return and set up a mobile clinic.

20

Chapter 3

GETTING PREPARED

'Unless the Lord builds the house, its builders labour in vain'.
'No branch can bear fruit by itself;
apart from Me you can do nothing'.
(Psalm 127:1 & John 15:4-5)

After two months back in England I was now ready to return to the mission field with my church's blessing and support. When my church prayed for me and 'sent me out', I was also given from my pastor a picture of footprints in the sand with the words *'Follow Me!'* How simple this sounds and yet it is the life of a disciple. How we want to know where, when, how and what will lie ahead of us if we choose to follow God. But it doesn't work like that in God's Kingdom. It really is about taking those steps of faith, obedience and following Him where He leads us - His timing, His way, and doing as He calls us to do. It is a step by step journey as we do His will each day!

This was exactly what Jesus said to His disciples and they had no idea what they were letting themselves in for. They just obeyed and followed Him, all the way to the cross. As a result they experienced His resurrection life and power like never before. This is still available for us today if we are willing to go *all the way* with Him. Where there is a death to our flesh, there is a resurrection life in our spirit. We need to let go of all our worldly desires and securities in order to enter into the fullness of the resurrected life He has called us to live with Him.

I asked God to provide a medical team to work with me in Africa and He gave me a picture. Instead of me going there with a team, I saw God bringing different people from other nations together and that we would meet up at the Iris base. I trusted Him and He was faithful, for this was just what happened.

God provides all you need for the work He calls you to do. I can testify to this after working for years in a richly resourced health service in England then taking a sudden 180 degrees turn to doing basic bush medicine in Africa. All that I took with me was my stethoscope, for He was going to provide whatever else was needed for the work that lay ahead.

Mission Impossible

My first challenge was getting a medical license to allow me to take medicines to the different rural villages. There were many obstacles and red tape I had to get through to get a simple license. I was first told by the Department of Health that I had to do voluntary work for one month in the main hospital in the Capital. I jumped over this hurdle when I explained I wasn't going to be doing hospital paediatrics but community medicine with a mobile clinic. They looked at each other puzzled, for they had never met anyone in my situation before and didn't quite know what to do with me.

I went through the various departments finding out their protocols for various community diseases and after three weeks, I ended up knocking on the Deputy's door. It seemed next to impossible to obtain a license and there was so much red tape it was unbelievable. I gave it to God realising this was His problem, not mine. If He wanted me to work in this nation, He needed to provide a license from their Department of Health to allow me to practice medicine here. I felt God was on my case, His favour was with me and I had to trust that He could make what seemed impossible, possible.

After three weeks, along with the help of another missionary, I finally received a document signed and stamped by the head of the Department of Health granting me permission to do voluntary medical work under Iris Ministries. In the natural this had all looked impossible, but with God nothing is impossible (Mathew 19:26). God shone His magnificent rays of light through the dark encompassing clouds, reminding me that I can do nothing without Him.

Spiritual Preparation

A Land-Rover vehicle had already been purchased and was being modified inside. Things weren't quite ready to start a mobile clinic so in the meantime I had been asked to sort out the clinic at the base. During this time, God was breaking me more and dealing with areas of my flesh that still had to die. He wasn't going to release me to do the mobile clinic until I was *spiritually ready* to take on such a job. Though we may think we are ready to take on specific tasks or roles, we may not be ready in God's eyes. The opposite is also true. We may not feel ready to take something on but in God's eyes, we are ready for the task. He knows when we are spiritually ready to step into what He has next for us.

While we need to do written and clinical exams to qualify to take on professional work in the world, in God's Kingdom it is different. We need to first know His character and have His Spirit dwelling in us. What we spiritually lack, He will give us for the work He has called us to do. After all, it is not by our might or by our own strength but by the power of His Spirit that we will succeed in what He has called us to do (Zechariah 4:6). This is a life of being transformed in our character and attitude so we can release a sweet and pleasing aroma to both God and man. God has made it so clear to me that character and attitude matter more to Him than our gifts and skills!

Medical Tent

Three months later when I was renewing my visa, it came to mind to purchase a medical tent for the mobile clinic. The lady I was staying with helped me find a good quality, hard wearing, army-like tent which would be our future clinic. *But how would I get these forty or more kilograms of equipment across the African border and onto a plane?* Thankfully, I didn't have to. God was already one step ahead of me.

I met somebody who 'just happened' to know someone who would be going by car all the way across the border to the Iris base. It would take them at least three days of travel and they happily took all the equipment in the back of their car. When I arrived back at the base the tent was less than ten metres away, actually next door waiting for me to pick up.

So we had a legal document of approval and a tent. Now we needed a team. In the meantime, along came another doctor, Eric, who was also at the mission school and had previously worked as a family doctor in Europe. And then along came a retired American nurse, Mary.

Eric had trained in General Practice and was a great blessing to have on the medical outreaches. We would split the clinic so he would see the men and I saw the women and children in each of the villages we visited. At other times we would share the load if one had more to see than the other.

Mary was also a great asset as she helped out with wound care and triaging the people. She also had amazing spiritual insight into the people she helped.

There were usually one or two members of the medical team on the medical outreaches. In addition to the core team there was the opportunity for visitors or mission school students who had an interest in healing the sick to join us on each outreach.

Giving Birth to Compassion

As well as being prepared on a practical level, it was equally (if not more) important to be spiritually prepared for each outreach.

One night I had a vivid, prophetic dream. I dreamt I was 38-weeks pregnant and about to go into labour. I knew this could not be possible apart from an immaculate conception. In shock I yelled, 'Stop!' and halted the labour. I woke up thinking, *'What was that all about?'* After discussing it with colleagues, I then realised my dream represented a 'spiritual pregnancy' where I was due to give birth to something spiritually. I had never heard of this before but other Christians around me had already experienced something similar. Just as we can give birth in the natural, we can also give birth to something which the Holy Spirit has sown in us in the supernatural.

Two weeks later (when I would have been 40-weeks pregnant), I felt like something inside me had to come out. It felt strange and I didn't know what was going on until someone prayed alongside me and then it felt like I was in labour. Funnily enough, this was not new to the person who was praying for me. She commented that she had been a 'spiritual midwife' before when praying for someone else in a similar situation. Tears flooded down my face and I wept feeling such a deep burden within. It felt like my spirit was groaning deep within and this came in waves like labour. I had never experienced this before but as it says in Romans, *'We do not know what we ought to pray for, but the Spirit Himself intercedes for us with groans that words cannot express. And He who searches our hearts knows the mind of the Spirit, because the Spirit intercedes for the saints in accordance with God's will'* (Romans 8:26-27).

After about forty minutes, it gradually came to a finish and I just felt exhausted after it all. I asked God, *'What was that all about? What had I given birth to spiritually?'* The answer was clear. It was His **compassion**! He said that I couldn't do the mobile clinic without this being birthed inside me for it is through His compassion that His healing will flow out to the people!

Team Unity

After God had spiritually prepared me, He showed me the team needed to be spiritually prepared before going on an outreach or mission. This was important so that there would be no opportunity or open doors to let the enemy in by means of witchcraft or sickness. Instead, we were to go out under the anointing and protection of the Holy Spirit. We were not to be deceived that just because we were good doctors taking free medicine into the villages we wouldn't come against spiritual opposition. For to some, we would be their enemies and they would be trying to get rid of us by whatever means!

As we were getting ready to start up the medical outreaches, a friend had a vision that she felt was for the medical team. She saw the medical team holding hands in a circle but the relationship was superficial or in the flesh. As a result, a swarm of mosquitoes transmitting malaria came and infected the team. However, when the team were locked together at the elbows, this tighter bond prevented the mosquitoes from attacking and they remained in good health. It was like being knit together at the elbows instead of holding loosely with the hands. This represented being united in the Spirit. I felt convicted by this that the medical team was to be united in the Spirit in order to prevent spiritual attack. Not only that but when brothers dwell together in unity, God blesses them with His oil of anointing (Psalm 133).

Team Preparation

There were four key areas that God pointed out to me to spiritually prepare each team before taking them out on a medical outreach. The purpose was so we could be united in His Spirit and His anointing could flow through each one of us.

1. Worship and entering the Presence of God.

This was vital. Worship helped us focus on Jesus and surrender our hearts, minds and wills to Him. We would open our hearts to be led by His Spirit in all we did, letting go of ourselves and worshipping before our King as we offered ourselves to do His Kingdom work.

During worship we would sense His amazing Presence and each time fall on our knees in awe of His Majesty. Many times there would be silence and a great sense of the weight of His Presence being right there in our midst. We would say nothing but simply enjoy Him being there with us. He would speak to us through pictures, His word, visions, prophecy and also by pouring out His love for each one of us. He was the Head of the team and we surrendered our natural skills and abilities to Him; for we couldn't do anything without Him and His Spirit flowing though us.

2. Prayer and intercession.

After we had come into His Presence through worship, we next entered into a time of prayer, giving Him thanks and praise and then inviting the Holy Spirit to lead us into the areas needing intercession. This ranged from praying for the people in the villages, especially those God wanted us to heal or reach out to, and also praying for the village chiefs. We would also ask God for words of knowledge or pictures of those whom He wanted us to specifically reach out and touch. We prayed against any spiritual opposition we felt we may encounter. We would also declare His

Kingdom come, His will be done, on earth as in Heaven and for God to create an open Heaven around us.

It was also important to pray a protective covering over our families and loved ones because when the enemy can't stop us bringing God's Kingdom from Heaven to earth, he will try and bring havoc to those we love. This is like a spiritual backlash. I have witnessed it happening on more than one occasion, but not so much after we prayed covering for our loved ones as well as ourselves. We would pray for His blood to cover us and His wall of fire to surround us as well as our families and loved ones.

3. *Feasting at His table (the Eucharist).*
This is an area I feel we don't give much attention to or the full credit it deserves. I believe taking communion regularly is a powerful and important part of every Christian's life, just like it was for the Apostles (Acts 2:42-46). During communion we would first ask the Holy Spirit to convict us of any sin or wrongful attitude. Then, as a team, we would come together as the Body of Christ and acknowledge Jesus as our Head.

It is through Jesus' blood that we can receive forgiveness, be cleansed, healed and set free. We dealt with any of our own spiritual or emotional problems first (things we needed to repent of or anyone we needed to forgive) so we were ourselves cleansed and healed before we started to minister to other people. It was also important to close any spiritual door we had opened up to the enemy through sin before we could set others free from any spirit of sin.

Just as Jesus laid His life down for us, we too offered our lives to Him and to serve Him in such a way that brought glory to His Name (instead of seeking our own glory). This was a powerful moment each time as it was done not out of duty but rather in awe and reverence to God. It also released a sense of honour and love to one another.

4. *Ministering and equipping one another.*
Finally we would pray for each other. These were great moments for everyone, now filled with the Holy Spirit, to give out words of encouragement, prophecy or simply pray as led by the Spirit for

one another. As the Spirit fell on everyone, we would see healing and deliverance as well as people being empowered and anointed under the power of the Holy Spirit. At the end, everyone would be anointed with oil and a blessing prayed on each in the Spirit. Many fell to the ground as the Spirit rested on them.

By the end of the evening the team would feel empowered, united in the Spirit and a sense of kinship to one another. Now we were ready, in expectancy and excitement of what our Heavenly Father was going to do through us.

On one occasion one of our core team members happened to arrive late at the end of the team prep meeting. I didn't want to exclude her but had a sense in my spirit that she shouldn't come for she hadn't been united in the Spirit with the rest of the team. I didn't have to say anything for she was immediately sensitive to the Holy Spirit and commented how she could see the spiritual bonding that had taken place in the team. She clearly saw that if she was to join the team having not been a part of the spiritual preparation, it would cause a disruption to the unity. This confirmed to me how important it was to spend these few hours together in prayer and worship where we truly were being bonded in the unity of the Spirit. This was to provide a supernatural protection over the team.

Many times, different people on the different teams witnessed that we were like little children holding onto our Father's arms going out to battle but being surrounded by His army of angels at our rear, ahead of us and at our sides. God was delighted that we were willing to co-labour with Him in the power of His Spirit and not rely merely on our own strength. With a few exceptions, the team was protected on every outreach and we experienced God's healing touch as we ministered in His power and anointing to His people.

Chapter 4

HOLY SPIRIT CONTRACT

'He called His twelve disciples to Him and gave them authority to drive out evil spirits and to heal every disease and sickness'.
(Mathew 10:1)

The first six months on the mission field were the toughest I encountered. I was constantly facing the temptation to return back to my medical career in England. I kept thinking, *'What have I done? How could I give up all my years of training and experience?'* I still had time to amend it all and get back into the profession if I chose to. But each time I entered the Presence of God, tears rolled down my face as He reminded me this was the cost to follow Him; this was what it meant to sacrifice my life for Him. So I let go of the negative thoughts the enemy was feeding into my mind and in return welcomed God's love and grace.

I was now in a time of transition. I was being 'derailed' from my former western way of medicine and stepping on an unfamiliar path not knowing where it was going. Though it wasn't easy, I decided to continue in faith and obedience to His Spirit.

In all of this, Jesus showed me that my sacrificial offering to Him of all my years of medical training and experience was like the poor widow's offering (Luke 21:1-4). What I had sacrificed to God was everything I had - though to Him, it was like a small gift for the King. God knows how much something has truly cost us when we have surrendered it to Him. He knows how much we have given by what we have left. God knows what sacrificial giving is all about for He sacrificed His one and only Son for us, so that we may personally come to know Him. He has already gone before us and asks us to do likewise. In return for my love offering, He was now going to show me things beyond my wildest imaginations. My spiritual contract was now unfolding as God further revealed His will for me.

Medical contracts state what the job expects you to be able to do and what experience you will gain from doing it. God's contract states what you will accomplish under the power of His Spirit but requires you to be willing to step out in faith and obedience.

What is our spiritual contract? Jesus refers to it specifically before He steps into His ministry. He declares that what had been written by the prophet in Isaiah (61:1-3) was now to be fulfilled. After laying down His career as a carpenter at the age of thirty, Jesus now stepped into the ministry work that God had prepared for Him to do. However, the following had to happen first.

'When all the people were being baptized, Jesus was baptized too. And the Holy Spirit descended on Him in bodily form like a dove. And a voice came from Heaven: **"You are My Son, whom I love; with You I am well pleased"**. *Now Jesus was about thirty years old when He began his ministry. Jesus,* **full of the Holy Spirit** *returned from Jordan and was* **led by the Spirit** *in the desert where for forty days He was tempted by the devil.... Jesus returned to Galilee in the* **power of the Spirit'** (Luke 3:21-4:19, summarized).

In order to begin fulfilment of His spiritual contract, Jesus first had to undergo His baptism in the river Jordan where He was *filled with the Holy Spirit*. During this time, His Father told Him how pleased He was for being His Son. Jesus had not yet entered His ministry but He knew His identity was in His relationship with His Father, not in what He did. He didn't have to earn this or achieve it - simply receive it.

Then Jesus was *led by the Spirit* into the desert for a time of testing. Usually, the things that God has revealed or challenged us with, or areas we have had to deal with in our life, will at some point be tested. It is very much like learning a subject and then being tested on it by means of having to pass a test or exam. So

God tests our hearts, to prove that we have understood and learnt from what He has taught us.

Jesus was first tested on His identity as the Son of God. We must know in our hearts and innermost beings our identity as sons and daughters of God before we step into any ministry work. This is an area we will constantly be tested in, for it is easy to let our work become our identity. Our spiritual authority comes from being God's children. Those who walk in spiritual authority know who they are as a son or daughter of the King. There is no questioning it in their hearts or minds.

Jesus had to also face trials and temptations in the areas of pride, power, status, idolatry, greed, as well as His flesh. After overcoming these tests and trials, He then graduated. He was now *anointed with the power of the Spirit.* He was ready to enter the work that God had ordained for Him to do, but now under an anointing!

It is at this point when Jesus reads out both His and our spiritual contract: '*The* **Spirit of the Lord is on Me**, *because* **He has anointed Me** *to* **preach good news** *to* **the poor**. *He has sent Me to proclaim* **freedom for the prisoners** *and recovery of* **sight for the blind**, *to* **release the oppressed**, *to proclaim the year of the Lord's favour*' (Luke 4:18-19).

Isaiah also adds, '*He has sent me* **to bind up the broken hearted,** *to* **proclaim freedom for the captives** *and* **release from darkness for the prisoners**, *to* **comfort all who mourn** *and provide for those who grieve in Zion- to bestow on them* **a crown of beauty instead of ashes, the oil of gladness instead of mourning, and a garment of praise instead of a spirit of despair** (Isaiah 61:1-3). Let us look in more detail at these verses.

The Spirit of the Lord is on Me, because He has Anointed Me

Jesus only entered His ministry when He had been anointed by the Holy Spirit to the work God called Him to do. Anointing means the power of His Spirit actually resting on us. This is the same as when Jesus told His disciples to wait in the city until they had been '*clothed with power from on high*' (Luke 24:49). This is like a mantle God gives us as we carry His authority and power for the missions and service He calls us to do. It's not for our personal use or gain but rather for the ministry He has called us to, which is for the benefit of others. We must humbly receive this and guard it from any form of pride or selfish ambition. People who carry an anointing are tempted to fall in sin through either a lust for money, fame, sexual temptations, pride or power. We must be on our guard to not give into such temptations. If we choose to daily lay down our lives to God and serve others in love and humility, then we will keep these temptations at bay.

To Preach Good News to the Poor

God has called us to reach out to the lost and poor in spirit with His love and compassion, telling them about Jesus and what He has done for them on the cross. It's telling them the Good News of the Kingdom of God and that Jesus has already paid the price for their sins. This applies to all of us for we all will meet those who don't know Jesus in our everyday lives. It's not just for the evangelists as I once thought. We are all called to be witnesses, telling others about the love of Jesus.

The poor are not just those who lack possessions or have nothing, but also those who do not know Jesus. Jesus said, *'You say, "I am rich; I have acquired wealth and do not need a thing." But you do not realize that you are wretched, pitiful, poor, blind and naked. I counsel you to buy from Me gold refined in the fire, so you can become rich; and white clothes to wear, so you can cover your shameful nakedness; and salve to put on your eyes so you can see. Those whom I love, I rebuke and discipline'* (Revelations 3:17). We are all called to reach out to the 'poor' in our community and share with them what the Lord has given us or done for us.

To Bind Up the Broken-Hearted

Jesus came to heal the wounded hearts. He came to heal those who are hurting both emotionally, mentally and spiritually. He wants to set us free from any grief, hurt, shame, trauma or pain that we have experienced, so we can move on in life and receive the fullness of His love that He has for us. God so wants to heal our hearts and make us whole again so we can live in a healthy, undivided relationship with Him and others.

A heart attack is when the heart muscle is starved from the oxygen it requires to maintain normal function. This usually occurs through a coronary artery (that is the blood supply to the heart muscle itself) being blocked. When we experience emotional pain in our life, unless we are able to deal with it in a healthy way, then we end up blocking off a part of our heart to God or others so it no longer functions the way it should. Only God can heal our hearts for He knows all that we have experienced in life, even the things we have blocked from our childhood memories because they are too painful to remember. I believe time simply suppresses our hurts instead of healing them. Otherwise, why does God so often take us back to the things in our childhood or earlier years in order to bring us to that place of healing and freedom? He has not only done this for me but for countless other men and women of God who are walking and living in His joy and freedom. It is one thing to be set free from demonic spirits but another thing to have our broken hearts healed. Only God can heal our wounded hearts with His power and unfathomable love.

At one point in my life, I experienced both betrayal and rejection from a colleague. When praying, a fellow prayer warrior saw in the Spirit what looked like a spear in my back. So she pulled the spear out of my back with prayer and, as she did, I felt immense pain within. It actually felt as if it was a real spear and I even sensed there was poison on the tip. A year or so later, I thought I had dealt with this wound after I had forgiven the person who had hurt me as well as dealing with any spirit of rejection attached to it. It wasn't until I experienced a similar situation, which triggered a deep hurt within, that I realised I still had a wound. On asking the Holy Spirit what was causing this emotional pain, He showed me that is was from the rejection I had felt previously. I thought that I had dealt with it. The truth was, I had dealt with the spiritual aspect but my wounded heart hadn't received the emotional healing it still needed. I suppose the spirit of both rejection and betrayal can be a likened to thorns or debris in a wound which need removing through repentance, forgiveness and renouncement. But the open wound itself still needs to be healed, with the soothing oil of His love and joy (Hebrews 1:9). It is His love that heals our wounded heart. As we let Him heal our hearts, we can then receive all the love He has for us and in return reach out to others with His love. He heals the broken-hearted and binds up their wounds (Psalm 147:3).

To Proclaim Freedom for the Captives

A captive can be someone who has been innocently imprisoned by another person's sin. They may feel like they are a prisoner of war. It may be that they have suffered some sort of physical, emotional or mental abuse through what someone else has said or done to them.

We can also be taken captive by the battle of thoughts that go on in our mind. We can become imprisoned by the beliefs or statements that we have said or heard others say. These are not from God but are from the world, flesh or the devil. Since Satan is the father of lies, they are false beliefs or false statements for they are not based on the truth of how God really sees us. Paul said, *'See to it that no one takes you **captive** through **hollow and deceptive philosophy**, that depends on **human tradition** and **the basic principles of this world**, rather than on Christ'* (Colossians 2:8).

We can make ourselves captives when we believe what the world or human tradition or culture says or the lies we hear from the enemy instead of accepting the truths which are from Jesus. Many people who are held captive by the lies they have believed are not even aware they are in captivity. The Holy Spirit needs to bring revelation to the truth so we can be set free from our captive minds.

To free captives is to free people from the negative experiences that others may have inflicted on them including curses, witchcraft, false guilt, false blame, lies, false beliefs, fears, control, betrayal, rejection and abandonment. It is also to set people free from the deception and lies they have believed and replace it with the truth of who they really are in Christ and as children of God.

Paul says, *'For though we live in the world, we do not wage war as the world does. The weapons we fight with are not the weapons of the world. On the contrary, they have **divine power** to **demolish strongholds**. We **demolish arguments and every pretension** that sets itself up **against the knowledge of God** and we **take captive*** *every thought to make it obedient to Christ'* (2 Corinthians 10:3-5).

We must choose not to live under the false beliefs, accusations or lies about who we are or what others say that is not from God but seek God for His truth. God will always reveal to us His truth if we ask Him how He really sees us or what the truth is in a given situation. We hear so many things each day which are not from God that we need to be able to filter them out. We can struggle to hear God if we don't take captive our thoughts. We can prayerfully take captive all thoughts and surrender them to God, commanding all that isn't from Him to leave. We need to seek God and ask Him for His truth and direction in all things. Paul said, *'Be transformed by the renewing of your mind'* (Romans 12:2). It is a daily choice to seek God and be led by His truth as we continue to renew our minds.

When I was seeking the Lord for healing over a particular issue in my life, I was surprised when He took me back to a time in my childhood. He brought to my memory the time when I was left by myself in a cot on a hospital ward. I was around one year of age with measles. Though I had no recall of this incident, the Holy Spirit revealed this memory to my spirit. In the memory, I felt abandoned and rejected and developed a fear of being on my own. Then I noticed a spiritual dark presence coming over my cot and I saw myself standing up in the cot crying. On realising this, I prayed and took authority over the spirits of abandonment, rejection, fear and loneliness and commanded them to go in the Name of Jesus. Then I asked Jesus where He was in this situation. Immediately, I saw Him come and pick me up and witnessed His light shining around me. Now, I could clearly see that I hadn't really been abandoned or rejected but it was a lie from the enemy because of the loneliness and fear I had felt. It was actually a false sense or perceived sense of rejection and abandonment. I then saw myself playing with Jesus and happily sitting in my cot with His Presence cloaked around me. I finally rebuked the lie that had fed into my mind and accepted the truth that Jesus will never leave or abandon me, even when I may feel alone. Jesus sets us free with the Word of His Spirit and His truth when we invite Him into our hearts.

On another occasion, I saw how my mind had been taken captive with a lie that my relationship with God was about achievement. The Lord showed me that I didn't have to achieve anything to be His child, but to simply have fun with Him. The need for achievement had been a familiar spirit that was in my family. The truth was that we are called to do God's will but do not need to seek after achievement in doing so.

To Release the Prisoners from Darkness

A prisoner is someone who is imprisoned as a result of the sin or crime they have committed. That means they are guilty for what they have done and would normally deserve punishment. It is only with God's mercy and love that we are forgiven and let off from the punishment that our sins deserve and hence released from any further imprisonment. Mercy is when God gives us what we don't deserve.

Jesus has already paid for us the price we owe for our sins. Being forgiven means being released of all guilt and punishment through what Jesus paid through His death on the cross for us. He has paid our ransom so we may join Him in His Kingdom. It is like Jesus coming to our prison cell with the key for the lock and saying, 'I have forgiven you and paid your debt. Come out'. Then we follow Him from the darkness that imprisons us into His amazing light and experience a true freedom within. We can each have this when we truly repent of our sins and choose to turn to Him. In doing so, we may need to also forgive ourselves or others for what they have done and by faith receive God's forgiveness for us.

We are imprisoned when we choose not to forgive. Jesus refers to this in the parable of the unforgiving servant. A man was in debt and owed his master much money. He begged his master to have mercy and not punish him for failing to pay back what he owed. The master went a step further and cancelled his debt and let him go. Then a fellow servant owed some money to this man who had been let off by his master. The fellow servant begged for mercy but the man chose not to forgive but threw him into prison until he could pay back his debt. When the master heard what this servant had done to his fellow servant, he withdrew his forgiveness and threw this man in prison. Jesus said that this is how God will treat us if we refuse to forgive others from our heart (Mathew 18:21-35).

Here God's forgiveness is what cancels our debt. Debt is referring to what we owe as a result of the sin we have committed and as a result, deserve to be punished or go to prison. If we are willing to forgive others and let them off the hook from owing us what they have taken from us, then God will forgive us and let us off the hook from owing Him anything. Forgiveness is the key that unlocks our prison door and sets us free.

When God called me to a war-torn nation in Africa, one of the things I ended up doing each week was visiting the local prison and reaching out to the prisoners with God's love, mercy, truth and healing power. Something God showed me was that the majority of the prison men had been brought up with little, if any, experience of a father's love. Their fathers had either died, weren't around or if they were around, they had beat them and were incapable of showing any love to them. When I asked if they wanted to know the Heavenly Father's love, nearly all their hands went up and tears were in their eyes. They repented of their sins and the crimes that got them in prison. They forgave their fathers for not being there or for beating them. Then we asked God to reveal His Father's love in a powerful and real way. The pastors who were with me went and embraced the men until they experienced God's love holding them. There was much weeping and the prisoners were like boys reaching out for their Father's love and acceptance.

It was a powerful time and a privilege to see God minister His Father's love to each man who was open to receive it. They were now experiencing an inner freedom and love like never before. The real prisoners were not those inside the prison walls, but those still in bondage wondering outside the walls.

Some of the men who received healing were actually released much sooner than their sentence. The authorities were able to see they had changed and were no longer a threat to society. Some of them left to become pastors in their home village for they wanted others back home to experience and know God in a real way like they now did. One prisoner was the son of a pastor, but had chosen the path of adultery and alcohol and through a car accident was taken to prison. It was in prison that he came back to his senses, like the prodigal son, and repented and wanted to get right with God. His father was praying that God would minister to him and transform his life while he was in prison. He too was released sooner than his sentence and went back to join his father in ministry. God wants to set the prisoners free but it has to start with our own hearts first.

Recovery of Sight for the Blind

God wants to open our eyes to see Him and be aware of His Heavenly realm. Deception, false beliefs and negative experiences in life stop us from seeing through clear spiritual lenses. We need to ask the Lord what has tinted or brought dirt to our lenses and stopped us from seeing Him clearly. Then repent of this and ask Him to open our eyes to see Him and all that He wants to reveal to us.

Elisha prayed, '"O Lord, open his eyes so he may see." Then the Lord opened the servant's eyes and he looked and saw the hills full of horses and chariots of fire all around Elisha' (2 Kings 6:17). God can heal our natural sight but, more importantly, we need our spiritual sight to be healed. All our natural senses (sight, hearing, touch or feel, taste and smell) are also spiritual senses where we can see, hear, smell, taste and feel in the Spirit. We can see life in the natural by what is going on around us or ask God to show us what is going on in the supernatural so we can see like Elisha's servant what is happening in the spirit realm. This can help guide our prayers or encourage us to see what God is doing in a particular situation.

To Comfort All who Mourn, Pouring on them His Oil of Gladness

To know His comfort is to experience His strength and Presence during difficult times in our lives. The word 'com-forte' means 'with strength'. Though mourning is a natural part of life, for some, it takes over their life and becomes like a toxin and stops them from moving on. I have seen peoples' faces change and become radiant as God ministers His Spirit of hope and gladness to them. He removes all sadness, grief and death, enabling them to start living their lives once again.

I experienced His comfort when my sister died of a genetic illness called cystic fibrosis. It was like a huge, warm soft blanket that His Spirit wrapped around me, but also gave me an inner strength to continue with my life, knowing that I would meet her in Heaven.

There was an African lady who came for treatment of her neck pain. It had started soon after her two children were killed by a drunk driver. She had since felt she couldn't carry on with her life. She was living in a daze and not able to think straight for herself or her other children. However, when she forgave the drunk driver and asked Jesus to heal her heart, not only did her neck pain instantly go but she also commented she felt she could start living her life again. She had been healed and freed from her pain and mourning and in return received His comfort and the oil of His gladness. She left the clinic with a smile on her face.

An elderly man had felt life wasn't worth living after his wife died. He too felt like he had undergone a death. After praying for him and breaking off the spirit of death and grief, he was able to see life through new lenses and felt an inner strength and joy to start his life afresh, not on his own, but now with Jesus.

To Give a Crown of Beauty Instead of Ashes

Ashes were marked on a person's forehead during a time of mourning or deep repentance. It usually went with tearing one's clothes or wearing sackcloth. Tamar put ashes on her head and tore her robes after she had been raped by her half-brother (2 Samuel 13:19). When Mordecai heard of the order sent out by Haman to destroy all the Jews, he tore his clothes, put on sackcloth and ashes and went out wailing loudly and bitterly (Ester 4:1). Jesus speaks of God's people repenting with sackcloth and ashes (Mathew 11:21).

It says in the book of Psalms, *'You turned my wailing into dancing; You removed my sackcloth and clothed me with joy'* (Psalm 30:11). God wants to restore and give back to us the inner beauty and joy that we lose when we experience sin, abuse or a death in our lives. He takes away the lifeless ashes and puts in its place a crown of beauty.

What the enemy has destroyed in our lives, God can take and resurrect again. He is able to give back life and beauty to what seems dead and lifeless. As we hand the things in our life over to Jesus, we let them die in the natural so He can transform them in the supernatural.

To Put on a Garment of Praise Instead of a Spirit of Despair
This is releasing people from depression and hopelessness into a place of freedom and joy where they can praise and worship God in spirit and in truth. It is like exchanging a cloak of despair and depression with a cloak of joy and praise. I have seen people under the oppression of the enemy but after praying, see them burst forth into spontaneous praise and worship. It was like seeing a light being turned on again.

One lady from an African village poured out her emotional distress to me as she shared about the many deaths that had taken place in her family. She was very distressed and had suffered much grief. The Spirit of God came upon me as I prayed for her and declared His oil of gladness upon her. She then started praising God and looked upwards with her arms raised high in the air. Her face now shone with such radiance you wouldn't have thought it was the same person. She was a testimony to the oil of His gladness replacing her mourning and to putting on a garment of praise instead of a spirit of despair. It was so beautiful to see.

A Shared Contract
After Jesus stepped into His ministry, He sent out His twelve disciples and instructed them to, *'Heal the sick, raise the dead, cleanse the lepers and drive out demons. Freely you have received, freely give'* (Mathew 10:8). Note that Jesus didn't say, *'pray for the sick'*, but instead He told His disciples to *'heal the sick'*. He was instructing them to do just as they had seen Him do. In Luke's account it says Jesus gave His twelve disciples *power and authority* to drive out *all demons* and to *cure disease, heal the sick* and preach the Kingdom of God (Luke 9:1-2). The disciples were given the same power and

authority that Jesus had to heal *all*. Instead of saying a prayer like, 'Jesus, can You heal them?', we are to pray with boldness, 'Be healed, in the Name of Jesus! Sickness go, in Jesus' name!'

Later Jesus sent seventy-two more to go into the towns and heal the sick. They came back with joy and said, '*Lord, even the* **demons submit to us in your Name**'. *Jesus replied, 'I saw Satan fall like lightning from Heaven. I have* **given you authority** *to trample on snakes and scorpions and to* **overcome all the power of the enemy;** **nothing will harm you**. *However, do not rejoice that the spirits submit to you, but* **rejoice that your names are written in heaven**' (Luke 10:17-20).

Jesus then sent report to John the Baptist of the healings and miracles taking place. '*Go back and report to John what you hear and see; the blind receive sight, the lame walk, those who have leprosy are cured, the deaf hear, the dead are raised and the good news is preached to the poor*' (Mathew 11:4-6).

This contract is for everybody! You don't need a medical degree or to be in the healing ministry to do it. You simply need to be filled with the power of the Holy Spirit and a hunger to do His will. His will is all of the above. The less we become self-focused and the more we become God-focused, He will give us His heart to reach out to the lost, free those who are captive, and heal the sick and suffering people throughout the nations.

A Loving, Compassionate and Willing Heart

We aren't to minister from a critical or judgmental attitude but instead a loving and compassionate heart that wants to see people set free, healed and restored. Jesus was willing to heal everyone who came to Him and asked for healing. He never refused or rejected anyone. Yet there were also moments when He spent time alone or with the disciples instead of tending the needs of the crowds. He simply did as He saw His Father doing and was not overcome by the needs of the people.

When I was working in Uganda in 2001, I remember how overwhelmed I would feel by the sheer number of sick children on the ward. I would feel a sense of duty to see them all but I realised this wasn't possible. I wasn't a superhuman doctor. Instead, I asked God to show me those He specifically wanted me to give medical attention to each day and I let the junior staff tend to the rest.

We all need to be guided by what we see God wants us to do and not what others demand from us. Otherwise, we can easily get burnt out and exhausted as we endlessly give out and are not spending enough time to fill up and rest in Him.

This is what Jesus came to do: seek the lost, destroy the works of the devil, heal the sick, set the captives free, raise the dead and take on the cross so we may experience resurrection life in Him. This too is what I believe our calling to follow Him is really all about.

Chapter 5

KINGDOM MEDICINE

'Praise the Lord, who forgives all your sins and heals all your diseases,
who redeems your life from the pit and crowns you
with love and compassion'
(Psalm 103:3-4)

It was now three months after I had arrived at the Iris mission base and we were finally ready to do our first medical outreach. Though this had seemed a long time of preparation and waiting, it was actually very quick by African timing. While I had been eager to start, I recognized that the preparation time was vital so we would be equipped in every way God wanted before we began.

On each mobile clinic, we had up to ten helpers including either students from the mission school or international visitors at the Iris base. Some were health workers; others simply had a passion to heal the sick.

Some villages were easy to get to, being just off the main road, and others required driving for hours off the road along uneven dirt tracks with numerous potholes or ridges. We were fortunate if there were any toilet stops along the way. Many times we would have to settle for the bush itself. It was all part of the adventure.

God is a God of adventures as it is exciting to follow Him to hidden places and meet people of different tribes, bringing them His love and healing Presence. It's then that the things of this world fade into the background. There is no comparison to seeing God's love and healing power at work among the poor, rejected and suffering people in this world. Suddenly, life takes on a new meaning as things fall into their true perspective. He will always give us His grace to do what He has called us to do, for we can only do it with His strength at work in us, not by our own strength.

As we arrived in each village, we were usually welcomed by the local people with singing and dancing in their tribal languages. Then we would meet the village chiefs or pastors. Most times we were warmly welcomed but on a few occasions we weren't. The places where we camped were usually at churches previously planted by Iris or they were new territories where the local pastor wanted to take us so the people who lived further out in the bush could be reached.

On one occasion, the church we visited was hidden behind the main road. I felt we would not be reaching the people in the village but just the few churchgoers. Then I noticed a marketplace nearby. The pastors had managed to get permission from the village chief to set up the clinic there. After we finished, the chief said there were more sick people that couldn't make it to the clinic and asked if they could be brought to church the next day. We agreed and did a clinic outside for the mums with their sick children. We prayed for them and gave out medicines where appropriate.

De-worming Children

Masses of children would congregate around our tents with protruding abdomens and wasted limbs. It crossed my mind to de-worm them all. God put it on my heart to pray for every child that we gave de-worming tablets to, that they would know His love, receive healing in their bodies and enter their callings and destinies. In some cases I felt led to bind evil spirits, especially the spirit of death, and would speak life over them instead. In other cases, it felt right to pray protection against any risk of abuse. This may be the only prayer some of them would ever receive but they were all precious to God. In a way, as a friend said, we were de-worming the children both physically and spiritually.

I'll never forget the scene when our car drove across an area of wasteland while heading for another small church. Hundreds of local children appeared out of nowhere and ran behind, following us all the way. As they ran after us they had such joy and excitement in their eyes. In the natural they wore filthy, torn clothes but in the supernatural I saw them wearing royal robes because they were actually His little princes and princesses.

One helper questioned what the point was in praying for them. Was this really going to have any effect in the long term? Then God showed her a picture. She saw a mass of bubbles with an electric light in each of them. Each bubble represented each child that had been prayed for. The bubble was God's protection on them and the light represented His Spirit in them. After receiving this revelation from God, the helper enthusiastically prayed for every child that came her way.

On occasions we ran out of de-worming tablets, but the children still wanted prayer. This was by far the more important of the two. On other occasions, when we clearly saw that there were more children than drugs, we prayed over the tablets that there would be enough. Sure enough, we always had enough down to the last tablet! We just kept giving out and not counting how many were left. It was such fun to see our Heavenly Father multiply the tablets. After praying for the children, they would instantly warm up to us so we would let them hang out and watch what we were doing.

Mobile Clinic
The next morning after our first night of camping, we would usually set up the clinic tent in a strategic location. We were flexible to the leadership plans which differed on each outreach.

The medical team would start by putting up the huge army-like tent. It was always a team effort requiring at least six people to lift the six poles up simultaneously as the tent was erected. Then, once the frame was up, the canvasses were attached to the poles. Lastly, the chairs and tables were assembled for the clinic inside. Before commencing we would pray together inside the tent. As we worshipped and prayed, God's Spirit would manifest in different ways each time. Sometimes there were outbreaks of holy laughter in the tent. On other occasions we could feel the wind of the Spirit moving amongst us. On one occasion, when a pastor came to join us in prayer, he was hit by the Presence of God and fell backwards within seconds of entering the tent.

Each time, we would claim the ground the tent was on to be holy ground and asked God to send His warrior angels, especially the angels ministering healing, salvation and deliverance. As the wind blew in from one end of the tent and out through the other, I would sense God's Spirit in our midst and His river of life flowing throughout. We prayed for anyone in the team needing the touch of God, including our translators. Then we were ready to start!

The tent was divided inside with material hanging across the middle of it so we had two clinics in operation with the people lining up on either side of the tent. We split the medical team up so there were people either working with myself on one side of the tent, or with a nurse or doctor on the other. Some were outside the tent helping to triage in the next person, or praying for the people outside while they were waiting. Local pastors or Bible school students would help with the translation and pray for the people in their tribal language. All in all, it worked out well each time and people were free to swap over during the course of the day. We usually worked until the sun was setting; then we finished and packed up everything before it was dark.

The medicines we had ranged from topical treatments for the various skin diseases, to a range of oral antibiotics, anti-malarials and analgesics, as well as many others. Commonly we treated people with scabies, ringworm, cellulitis, burns and wound infections as well as purulent conjunctivitis, chest infections, urinary tract infections (including schistosomiasis), malaria, dysentery, giardia, and non-infective ailments like acid-reflux and constipation.

In some villages there was a common theme of symptoms among the sick, ranging from chest infections to dyspepsia to chronic generalised body aches. It was interesting to discern whether this was due to natural causes, dietary problems or possible curses on the village.

God was teaching me on each outreach more Kingdom medicine. I was seeing that the tent was more than a clinic but was actually representing His tabernacle, where people could come in and find safe refuge and get healed.

Witchcraft

On my very first encounter with a village woman, it entered my mind to ask if she had been to the witchdoctor. I questioned why God wanted me to ask her this, for what good was it going to be? But I did ask her and she replied yes. *'Now what?'* I thought. God replied, *'Bring her into My Kingdom and tell her about Me'*. So I did! I was surprised how this woman, who had never heard of Jesus, was willing to say she was sorry for her sins, then invite Jesus into her life and ask Him to heal her. After she did this, I said a prayer and we tested the affected part of her body. She appeared completely healed. All her body pain had gone and she had full movement with her body. There were many more cases similar to this of witnessing healing when the powers of witchcraft were broken and people turned from witchcraft to Christ.

One man of nearly ninety years of age had an itchy body for nearly twenty years. On examination, his skin looked in good condition for his age. On further questioning, he had been to the witchdoctor many times. After he repented and renounced the power of witchcraft, he asked Jesus to heal him. His body was completely healed. Not only had the itch gone but he testified to having an inner warmth throughout his body as he was experiencing the healing power of the Holy Spirit. He had no idea the itch was a result of witchcraft.

There was a similar case of a man who experienced an intense itch after certain people passed his home. These people practiced witchcraft. When he understood that he had spiritual authority over demonic spirits, the next time the itch started he rebuked it in the Name of Jesus. When I saw him again, he testified with a smile on his face that it immediately left him.

During a mobile clinic, there was a lady who came wearing little on the upper part of her body. What she wore looked torn to shreds and only fit for the bin. As she looked at me, I saw much fear and darkness in her eyes. Her problem was her left arm. It was shaking at a rate of at least three tremors or shakes per second and she could not stop it or control it. As she held it, the shakes continued. On further questioning, I found that her arm suddenly started shaking one night about eighteen months ago and had stayed the same ever since. I asked if anything significant happened in her life just before the tremor started. She commented that she had been at a ceremony in her village the day before and came across one of her enemies. She may have cursed them and they probably cursed her back or went to the witchdoctor to put a curse on her. Also, it was in the middle of the night when much witchcraft activity takes place. It seemed pretty likely that she had been involved in witchcraft one way or the other. This lady didn't know Jesus but I explained who He was and that He could heal her arm. She was too afraid to accept Jesus (and I could see by the intense fear that was in her eyes), so I simply prayed for His peace to come and be with her. She smiled as she received His peace and then said she wanted Jesus in her life. She repented of all witchcraft activity and forgave others for cursing her. She then asked Jesus into her life and to restore her arm to normal function. She now had a peaceful look on her face since the fear had left her, but there was still no change in her arm. I was convinced this was due to witchcraft or some demonic spirit and expected to have seen more healing results by now. I asked her if she could wait outside the tent. An hour later, she was noted to have a reduced tremor rate of around one tremor per second. She was smiling, noting the improvement. By two hours, just as we were finishing clinic, her arm was completely healed! I can only say that she was either in the *process* of being fully healed or, by hanging out in the Presence of God, she received full healing. I will let you decide.

I saw many people being set free from the effects of sin and witchcraft and receive physically healing. Also, how salvation, deliverance and healing are all part of a spiritual package that God has for each of us. There is no formula as such, but a simple understanding that when people surrender their lives to Jesus and renounce any involvement in witchcraft, He heals them and sets them free!

We have an amazing God who has already sent His one and only Son to pay the price for ALL of our sins and take ALL of our sickness and diseases on the cross. As it says in the book of

Psalms, 'Praise the Lord, who *forgives all your sins* and *heals all your diseases*, who *redeems your life* from the pit and crowns you with *love and compassion*' (Psalm 103:2). Jesus came to heal and set free *all* who were brought before Him (Mathew 4:23, 9:35). He never refused anyone who came for healing whether it was for someone else or themselves.

Chronic Body Pain

There were many people who came to our clinic complaining of chronic body pain, usually all over from their necks down to their ankles. This may have been due to natural reasons from repeated stress on their bodies from manual labour, but I believe a lot was also due to the effects of sin and witchcraft. Where it was appropriate I would lead the people in repentant prayer and to renounce the effects of witchcraft on their bodies, followed by the inviting of Jesus into their hearts. They would then get up and test their bodies and really stretch their affected parts. The result would be watching them exercise their bodies with smiles on their faces. For those who were partially healed, they would receive more prayer. We simply asked God to complete what He had started and they would be some degree better if not fully healed. Due to time and people waiting, I prayed no more than three times per person for those who were partially healed and trusted God to complete the work.

Some were instantly healed; others were healed as they stepped out in faith by exercising the affected part of their body. Others were healed in the hours that followed or even the next day or week. It was our job to pray in faith with compassion and trust God to heal when He chose to. We would encourage the people to test their affected body part and I saw many step into healing as they did this. Jesus demonstrated this when He told the paralysed man to hold out his hand or the cripple man to get up. As they **took action** they were healed (Mark 2:11). When Jesus told the lepers to go to the priest, it was **as they went** they were healed (Luke 17:14).

One old lady had seen her long term friend, who had been crippled with pain and unable to carry anything, carrying water once again from their well. She was surprised and asked her what had happened. Her friend testified to receiving prayer and healing from the clinic and pointed her in our direction. So she came to the clinic in faith that God would heal her like He did her friend. She too had chronic body aches but also ringing in her ears and complained of 'dark vision'. I prayed for her pain to go and she too received complete healing. Then, when I offered to pray for her hearing and vision, she looked at me as if to ask why. It was already healed. God just did it all in one go. He heals however He chooses and can do it all at once!

Many times when people complained of pain in different parts of their bodies, I would find on examination no signs to suggest it being organic in nature. Then I would be led to break off any witchcraft or curses and command the spirit of infirmity to leave in Jesus' Name. You knew when it was spiritual or demonic because the pain would shift to a different part of their body or get worse with prayer. Others would comment after prayer that they felt something 'leave their body' along with the symptom also going. This is very different to 'referred pain' which is organic in nature and usually stays in the same referred place. For example, a person may have a medical problem in their right hip but pain is 'referred' from the right hip to the right knee. The person then thinks it's their knee that has the problem, until the doctor examines and finds the problem is coming from the hip. Doctors are aware of this type of organic referred pain.

Some people testified that after receiving prayer the affected part of their body went from feeling hot to cold then back to normal. Others felt their body go heavy then light. Some would describe a warmth over the area being healed. We would continue in prayer until the affected part of their body felt normal again.

One lady who had already accepted Jesus in her life had pain in her chest which moved from her left to right side when being prayed for. I told her that since now she was a believer she had the authority of Jesus to command it to leave and not return. She told it to go in Jesus' Name and it instantly left her body.

Another lady had pain in her chest and breast, yet examination was normal. After we prayed and took authority over it in Jesus' Name, it too completely disappeared.

Compassion Releases Healing

As I listened to different peoples' problems and sufferings I felt varying degrees of compassion for each one of them and prayed God's love and healing power to come and touch them. Whenever I felt an overwhelming amount of compassion towards an individual, I would also feel the power of the Holy Spirit touch them as I held their hands and prayed for them. I would know in my spirit they were being healed whether they were able to immediately demonstrate it or not.

On one occasion an old lady with chronic body pain said she felt no different after I prayed for her. Then to my amazement the Holy Spirit convicted me and said, *'You didn't pray with compassion!'* My mind had actually been focused on other things when I prayed for her, so I repented of not engaging my heart. Then, when I prayed a second time with my heart engaged, she was healed of all her aches. What a lesson on compassion and healing! The Holy Spirit was right on my case and I couldn't afford to pray without His compassion. Jesus had compassion on all those He healed. I believe that is why He birthed it in me before He let me step into doing the mobile clinics.

Witchdoctor Healed

A witchdoctor came into the clinic. He came into my colleague's side of the tent and it just happened that my colleague for this outreach was a visiting surgeon. The witchdoctor was an elderly man with visual impairment most likely due to cataracts. He had tried his own remedies and potions but with no improvement. When my colleague asked him if he had been to the witchdoctor, the translator replied quietly with his hand part over his mouth that he *was* the witchdoctor. The witchdoctor was then told about the healing power of Jesus and that He could restore his sight but he needed to choose to step into God's Kingdom, which meant leaving his spiritual powers of darkness behind. After five minutes (and many of us silently praying for this man's salvation), the witchdoctor agreed. It was amazing what happened next. My colleague led him to Jesus and he renounced his witchcraft practices. We prayed Jesus would not only physically restore his sight but open his eyes to see Jesus and His amazing power. He next looked out of the tent and commented that he could clearly see the trees in the distance and the people passing by. He smiled testifying to God restoring his vision! Not only that but we could now see a light and radiance coming out of his eyes instead of the darkness which was there before. The witchdoctor asked my colleague what he should do with his potions and remedies that he used to kill people. He was told to destroy them all and never use them again. We then found the local pastor and introduced him to this new brother in Christ.

There were other occasions when we had witchdoctors enter our tent, but they just wanted medicines and no prayer. They sadly left with fear in their eyes when we explained Jesus' power to heal and set them free. They were not only afraid of the power of the Holy Spirit, but also of the consequences if their 'colleagues' who also practiced witchcraft found out.

The Blind See

I was surprised in one village where three people came into the clinic who were all blind. I felt like telling them they had come to the wrong clinic. I wasn't an ophthalmologist and had no medicines to heal their sight, but they all came expecting to somehow get their vision restored. All I had to offer them was Jesus.

The first was a young girl who had difficulty seeing. Her mum said she was blind, but this was difficult to assess for the girl was unable to co-operate with me. After praying for her, I got the girl to count my fingers. She quietly said there were four fingers and a thumb. Then she was able to reach for my stethoscope. Her mum said she couldn't do this before. So, there was some degree of healing though it was difficult from examination to know how much she was impaired and could now see. However, there was a happy mum and a smiling little girl.

Then along came an old lady with opacities over her eyes. We prayed for her vision and she seemed to be able to see pretty well in the distance. She too was smiling and laughing by the time she left.

Our final lady was brought in with the aid of her little children. She was indeed totally blind, unable to get about on her own, and moved her ears to the sound of others speaking. She had to feel her way through the tent, holding onto her children's hands for guidance. On asking how it happened, she said it was a sudden onset. One day she was fine, the next day completely blind. Her eyes looked glazed over. Since I am not an ophthalmologist I was unsure if this was the result of some acute medical cause. She said she had not been able to see for two years. As we prayed for her sight to be restored, we broke off any curse or witchcraft that could have been behind it and asked Jesus to open her eyes to see again. She smiled and said she could now see something. She no longer saw darkness but could see light and colours.

We prayed a second time thanking Jesus for what He had started and asking Him to complete it. She smiled even more with excitement in her face saying her vision had improved and she was now seeing objects, though they were still a blur. With the excited look on her face our faith soared as we prayed a third time. This time I felt led to pour anointed water (water which has been prayed over and blessed in Jesus' Name) over her eyes. What happened next I will never forget. On asking her what she could see, she said she could clearly see what was outside the tent, commenting on the trees and people around. Then she noticed I was wearing glasses and enthusiastically looked around at everyone in the tent pointing to what she could now see. Here was one extremely happy, excited woman who could now truly see again. It was marvellous watching her leave the tent unaided, able to see where she was walking, with her children happily following her. We all looked at each other in utter amazement and awe of what we had just witnessed God do. We were speechless thinking, 'Did you see that?' It is true… He restores sight to the blind!

Villages of Other Faiths
We hit another village, but this time it was a community who were of another faith.

One man received healing after deciding to invite Jesus into his heart. He amazed me with what he said next. 'We need a church in this village!' he confidently exclaimed. He must have had such an encounter with God and revelation of His love that he wanted others to receive it too.

Then we had two men who came into the clinic together. We normally see people individually but for some reason it seemed okay they came in together. The first man had generalized chronic body aches but didn't want to receive Jesus in his heart. We gave analgesia but said this wouldn't heal him in the long term. Then he sat and watched his friend.

His friend was quite sick and simply wanted to be healed. He didn't mind how this would be, so he was willing to receive Jesus as his Lord and Saviour. After praying for him, he checked out his body and said he felt his normal healthy self again. He was completely healed. We smiled and, as we were saying goodbye, his friend jumped back onto the chair. He responded to the testimony of his mate being healed right in front of him and he wasn't going to leave until he got the same. He now was ready to receive Jesus and sure enough his chronic aches left him. He too left healed and happy.

One teenage boy came with a chest infection. He was coughing with chest pain. He decided to accept Jesus and was instantly healed. I wanted to confirm this by listening again to his chest but he blatantly remarked, 'It's gone!' I was even going to give him antibiotics but he looked at me and said he really didn't need it, for he knew he was completely healed. He looked at me with a serious look in his eyes and said that he was now going to pursue God and serve Him. I was stunned and encouraged him to do this. He then enquired about going to a church. We directed him to a group of teenage children who loved Jesus and happened to be worshipping together nearby. This boy received his call when he encountered Jesus and experienced His love and healing power. What a joy to see.

Deliverance with No Manifestations
One amazing thing I noted time and time again was that the people whom I saw healed in the tent showed no demonic manifestations. Even the witchdoctor who was healed sat still. It was only the countenance in his eyes and face that changed from exuding darkness to radiating light. *How could this be?*

One thing I had feared with deliverance ministry was if people threw themselves or lashed out at me when being delivered. This was one of the initial reasons I hadn't wanted to ever get involved in deliverance ministry. But this just didn't happen in the tent. One person, who had been demonically manifesting by shaking their body when being prayed for outside the tent, stopped shaking when brought into the tent. They were healed without any further manifestation seen.

I pondered on this and asked God why we didn't see it happen in the tent when I knew people were being set free and delivered of evil spirits. The reply was that because it was a clinic, God was choosing to honour this. It was also His tabernacle, where His Presence and His glory were being displayed. The very fact that we worshipped in it, claimed the ground, and welcomed His Presence and mighty warrior angels made it a place for people to feel safe to enter and have an encounter with Him. This also protected those who were waiting outside from any fear arising if they were to hear manifestations coming from inside. What was being witnessed instead was people entering sick and leaving healed. Their physical healings bore testimony to the people around who knew them. This in turn raised people's faith to come to the clinic, because they knew they had a chance of being healed. This was how God did it and I liked His style!

We did see some people demonically manifest *outside* the tent but not when people were set free from witchcraft and evil spirits *inside* the tent. The most I witnessed were tears streaming down their face or eyelids blinking fast. They testified after to feeling things leave their body or changes in body sensations. I would see changes in their eyes. One minute they would appear to be exuding what looked like darkness and evil, to later seeing light and joy radiating out. It was amazing. This is what is meant by the eye being a gate or lamp to the soul. When your eye is bad (or evil looking) it reflects the darkness within you and when your eye is good, it reveals the light inside of you (Luke 11:34).

Sometimes people have not been able to look at me when they have needed some sort of deliverance. Their eyes have been all over the place. I realised it was the demon in them not wanting to come face to face with the Spirit of God in me. After they had been set free, they were able to look me in the eye with no problem.

One evening, when the clinic had finished and the team joined in praying outside for others, I was drawn to a lady who appeared to be holding herself back from going forward for prayer. Her body looked tense. When my friend and I went over to offer prayer for her, she pointed to pain in her back. After we prayed, she was able to bend her back and it looked a bit more flexible. My friend had the impression there were deeper emotional issues that also needed prayer, so she started praying for the lady. As she did, the lady started to demonically manifest. She rolled her eyes back and screamed out uncontrollably while arching her back and neck. She then started to lose consciousness. I embraced the lady and commanded the spirit to be quiet in Jesus' Name. I then called the lady back to full consciousness in the Name of Jesus. She came around a few minutes later and at that point I asked her if she would like to invite Jesus into her heart. She immediately said yes. After we led her to Jesus we then led her in prayer to renounce the demonic spirit, commanding it to leave in Jesus' Name. She did and then followed by inviting the Holy Spirit and love of Jesus into her heart. I noted that by approaching it this way, she was set free *without* any more manifestations. She smiled at the end and could now fully move her body in all directions with no more tension or pain!

I believe we can minimise any demon manifesting itself as it leaves a person's body, if a person accepts Jesus as their Lord and Saviour first. They themselves are then in a position where they can bind the demon and command it to leave. Otherwise, the manifestation continues when the demon is fighting to stay in their body because the person hasn't yet commanded or authorised the demon to leave. Once they have accepted Jesus as their Lord and Saviour, they now have the authority to renounce any demon. When they tell it to go, its time is up and it has to go.

The Lame Healed
One evening, after we had finished the mobile clinic, I hung around the periphery of a group of local people. There I noted a small, old lady hobbling with a bamboo stick, needing physical

support from others. I decided to approach her and asked if I could pray for her. I had no interpreter so communicated using sign language. She agreed. She was a woman of another faith and had just watched (along with a crowd of others) the Jesus Film. Here I prayed for her healing without primarily leading her to Jesus since I had no translator. I then took her stick from her and got her to walk. As I took her hand, she was at first very wobbly, but gradually her steps became more balanced and steady. Then her steps became normal. I let go and told her to run... and she did! There was laughter and outcries around as people witnessed her getting healed. The pastor witnessed her healing and broke her stick. Though she was of another faith, her Christian family had been praying for her salvation. The pastor asked if she wanted to accept Jesus there and then. She wasn't ready and had to think about it but smiled since she had been healed. This released faith for the rest of the crowd to step forth and receive healing too that night.

On another outreach, an old lady was carried in on the shoulders of four men. She had suffered for years with chronic pain throughout all her body. It was so bad that she was now unable to walk and continually felt frail and weak. I asked if she knew Jesus. She said she did and also believed He could heal her right then. I declared healing throughout her body, breaking off any spirit of infirmity. I asked her to stand up and hold my hands. She did and began to walk with me in the tent. Next, she jogged on the spot with me. I then waved bye to her as she walked out unsupported from the tent! It seemed so simple! Yet, that's how God works. He knew her heart and faith to get healed. So He did it and she stepped out into it.

There was a very old, wrinkly lady who walked in with a staff in her hand. She expressed such relief in her face as soon as she made it inside. She said she saw power coming out of the tent and could see it was 'good power'. It had actually been a struggle for her to physically get to the tent for the enemy didn't want her to come. She said that evil power was holding her back. She was so relieved when she made it inside. She explained how she had been under the power of the witchdoctor for years through having a relationship with him. She didn't like it but saw no alternative, until she saw the 'good power' radiate from our tent. She had been waiting for a long time to get free from him, thinking there must be something better. As soon as I told her of Jesus and asked if she wanted to know Him, she adamantly said 'Yes!' and nearly blew me back. She really did want Him and had been waiting for years to find this alternative good source of power. She boldly renounced any witchcraft and gladly welcomed Jesus into her life. She had come with red, painful, weeping eyes and pain down one side of her back and leg. The pain left her body, including her eyes, so I only had to give some eye drops for the redness. She was one happy woman, set free from Satan's clutch and now under the power of the Holy Spirit. She kept thanking Jesus as she experienced such joy and freedom in her life. She said she was now going to tell people in her village of God's power. I could see her doing this for she was a woman with authority, like an elder. She was obviously not going back to the witchdoctor but going to testify to others about Jesus! What a privilege to pray for her.

Forgiveness Releases Healing

On a trip with my church to Zambia, I met an old man who limped in with a walking stick. He had been limping for nearly forty years as the result of a car crash. He came for more analgesia and told me he was a Christian. I asked if he had forgiven the person who injured him. The answer was no. *Was he willing to?* Initially his facial expression asked, 'Why should I?' After all, it was the drunk driver's fault. But it's the kindness of God that leads to repentance (Romans 2:4).

After lovingly explaining that God releases His healing power when we choose to forgive, he gave out a deep sigh and decided to do it. He repented for his bitterness and unforgiving heart and chose to forgive the person who caused his disability. He then asked Jesus to heal and restore his leg. I took the stick from him and asked God to reverse what had happened to his leg in the Name of Jesus. After instructing him to get up, I held his hand and he got up to walk. He not only walked - he ran. He left the clinic physically healed, emotionally and spiritually set free with his walking stick held over his shoulders. Forgiveness brings physical healing as well as spiritual and emotional healing.

A local lady came to our African church and specifically asked for prayer for her abdominal pain. She had been having stomach aches for two weeks with no diarrhoea or vomiting and no other accompanying gastro-intestinal symptoms. She had been to a witchdoctor at some point in her life. We first prayed against the witchcraft and spoke healing to her abdomen, but she felt no better. Then I thought there may be a curse on her, so we broke any curse. She felt worse after this. (The fact she was feeling worse with prayer made me think it was spiritually related.) Next, I asked if there was anyone she needed to forgive whom she didn't like or felt resentful towards. She nodded, yes. It had been the same time when she fell out with this person that her symptoms started. She forgave and let go of the person who had hurt her. This time her abdomen was healed. She said she felt something leave her abdomen and felt a lightness inside with no more pain. I believe there was a spirit of unforgiveness behind her abdominal pain and it left as soon as she dealt with it.

On another occasion, a staff member asked me for medicine for his wife who was at home with 'renal' pain. On further questioning, the pain seemed muscular and chronic and not necessarily renal in origin though it appeared in the loin area. I got him to ask her if she needed to forgive anyone. Yes, her mother! So at home she prayed with her husband and forgave her mother from all the things she had said and ever done to her. Then her loin pain disappeared. I didn't even see this woman or pray for her. She just responded to the advice and after forgiving her mother, was healed.

This is the power of forgiveness. I have seen so many cases when people choose to forgive their enemies or those who hurt them and they themselves are then set free and healed. It is not about whether the perpetrator or offender deserves to be forgiven. God is the only judge who can make that decision. If we choose not to forgive then we ourselves will become victims to hatred, anger, resentment, bitterness, judgement and unforgiveness. This in turn can become like a toxin which attacks our body, causing physical ailments.

James says that the tongue is a restless evil, *full of deadly poison* (James 3:8). I have seen people with swollen and even twisted joints who were full of bitterness and hatred to others but, the moment they forgave those who hurt or offended them and repented of their wrongful attitude, their joints got healed. As we decide to let our offenders off the hook so they no longer owe us anything, we ourselves end up being set free and healed. I believe that's how it works.

One lady I met in the UK had painful arthritic joints and asked me to pray for her. Before I did, I asked her if she needed to forgive anyone who had offended her. She at first said no, then immediately was convicted by the Holy Spirit of her mother-in-law. After she repented of her negative feelings to her mother-in-law and forgave her of how she had mistreated her, we then prayed for her joints to be healed. She sat on the floor and, for the first time in ages, could now get up with ease from the floor. Her joints were completely pain free. She commented that she hadn't been able to do that in a long time and had never thought that the two were related.

It is important to find out what happened in someone's life around the time they started to get sick or have body or joint pain. There may have been an unpleasant experience that led to them feeling hurt or becoming bitter or angry and that in turn has now become the root cause of the symptoms in their body. It may be that the person has cursed themselves or hates themselves and spoken bad words to themselves. They need to repent and forgive themselves and in return bless themselves.

Proverbs says how our attitude and what we speak will influence our bodies and health. It says that if we *'fear the Lord and shun evil'* this will **'bring health to your body and nourishment to your bones'** (Proverbs 3:7-8). Also, **'A heart at peace gives life to the body but envy rots the bones'** (Proverbs 14:30). Likewise, **'A cheerful heart is good medicine but a crushed spirit dries up the bones'** (Proverbs 17:22). We must learn from these proverbs for there is profound truth and wisdom in them regarding how our emotions and spirit affect our health, especially our bones!

I met a lady with chronic hip pain who was prayed for but the pain remained. On questioning if she needed to forgive anyone, she said no and that she had forgiven all her enemies. I was somehow convinced she hadn't. This time I asked her if she had forgiven them from her heart. She then admitted that she hadn't. After she decided to do this, we prayed for her hip to be healed and the pain completely went.

Jesus said we are to forgive others if we want our Heavenly Father to forgive us of our sins but we are to forgive from our *heart* (Mathew 18:35). To forgive from our heart is when we can imagine ourselves giving our offender a hand shake or a hug or inviting them for a drink (even when they don't deserve it) and releasing them from owing us anything. Sometimes it is not enough to just say 'I forgive'. We have to really mean it and let go of all the things they have said or done that have offended or caused us pain. We need God's amazing grace to do this. If we ask Him for it, He will give it to us; that is, the spiritual strength and ability to reach out to our enemies with His love for them.

You may say that you can't possibly forgive a person for what they did to you, but Jesus did. He was betrayed by His own men, mocked, spat upon, slandered, physically beaten and tortured to the point His body was bruised, bleeding and disfigured. Jesus said on the cross, '*Father forgive them, for they know not what they are doing*' (Mathew 23:34). I believe, with the same grace that Jesus had, we too can choose to forgive those who have badly hurt us. We always need to choose to forgive and be at peace with others to keep ourselves whole and free from any spirit of bondage that comes along with unforgiveness. Forgiveness cleanses us of toxins to our body and heals our bones.

Fetishes

I didn't know much about fetishes until they were pointed out to me by the pastors and local African people. Fetishes are pieces of string or cord tied around the sick part of the body (usually the neck, waist, ankles or wrists) forming a band. They also may have knots in them. They are received from the witchdoctor or may be a 'present' from a relative with the belief that by placing them around the affected part of the body, it will get better. Those worn around the neck usually have a small sack attached to them with medicines or herbs inside and look like a necklace. I initially found it hard to believe that such things could possess power, but the truth is they actually do contain evil power and need to be broken in the Name of Jesus and destroyed, usually by burning. For some, they were a present from a relative so they didn't want them removed. But the people we saw who were still sick usually took our advice and had them removed. We never removed them without their permission.

One helper, whilst praying for a lady, sensed there was power around her waist. She was fully clothed and when we asked to look at her waist, there was a fetish around it! She allowed us to remove the fetish and pray for her abdomen. She then received healing.

There was a baby who was brought to me, looking quite sick. I noticed fetishes around his neck, waist, arms and legs. I didn't note any specific signs to suggest organic illness on examination. The mother agreed to have the fetishes removed and we prayed for the baby to be healed and set free from any spirit linked to them, especially the spirit of death. A few minutes later, there was a change in the baby's appearance. The baby now looked happy, was playful and active, and seemed a normal healthy child. Everyone in the team agreed and the mother even laughed and smiled. This was the enemy's power broken over this baby and the receiving of life and health which was declared. I had never witnessed anything quite like this before in all of my paediatric training.

We usually burnt the fetishes at the end of an outreach, taking the advice of the local pastors and also so that they couldn't be re-used by anyone else. On one occasion, a fetish would just not burn. After we broke the evil power over it in the Name of Jesus, it ferociously set on fire!

Cursed Village

In one village, the people all presented to the clinic with the same problem. Some were children, others were young adults or older people. Regardless of their age, they all had some degree of generalised body pain which affected mainly their limbs and joints. For all of them it had lasted for the past two months! It suddenly came to mind that these people could have had curses spoken over them around two months ago by someone that may have cursed the village. There was no medical explanation for all the different ages to have pain in their joints and back with no other medical symptoms (such as fever, malaise, sore throat, rash, diarrhoea, etc.), especially since they all seemed relatively well on examination. I suddenly informed my colleague of what the Lord had shown me. We broke off the curses over each person in Jesus' Name and blessed their bodies with His peace and love. Everyone we prayed for was instantly, completely healed. On that occasion I ended up giving out very little, if any, medicines for they all simply got better when the curse had been broken off them.

Other Curses

On one occasion I went with a friend to get a cool, refreshing drink when I suddenly developed an intense band of pain around my head. The pain level was gradually increasing and felt like someone was tightening a metal band around my head. I had never experienced such head pain and instantly knew I was being cursed. My friend prayed for me and broke the curse. The pain started to go down and left as quickly as it came.

Another lady came to me with a two month old baby. One day she was breastfeeding fine; the next day she had no milk. It just stopped. She was a well-built lady and her breasts also well-developed. I examined her and, sure enough, no milk came out of either breast. I found her story hard to believe until it came to my mind that this may be due to a curse. She repented of going to the witchdoctor and I broke any curses off her breasts. I spoke blessings over her and for milk to flow forth again. She tested one breast and out squirted milk. She looked excited then tested the other. Milk also came out. Tears welled up in her eyes. As simple as the curse came on her, it was easily broken off her in the powerful Name of Jesus and replaced with a blessing.

During another clinic, an old-looking lady presented with a history of weight loss, no appetite, no thirst and feeling very weak and lethargic. On examining her, there was nothing to find to suggest any serious illness including no signs of significant anaemia, enlarged organs or abnormal masses. Her examination was actually normal apart from her looking very lethargic and oppressed. I asked her if anything happened around the time she started to waste away. She said she had been to a ceremony and openly admitted that she had been cursed by someone and then deteriorated after that. With no further explanation, she was willing to forgive her enemy and ask Jesus to forgive her. We broke off the spirit of death and any curses spoken over her and declared life and health in the Name of Jesus. Then we tested her body out. She was actually able to walk unaided for a fair distance. When she came back, she had no difficulty eating a sandwich and could drink water in a normal fashion. I told her she wasn't going to die but live, for the curses were now broken and we had spoken blessings over her. This was a lady who admitted only when questioned that she had been cursed and had deteriorated since then. We then reversed it by praying blessings to her body and declaring health and life over her.

Darkness of Vision

It was interesting that on many other occasions people would come to me complaining of having 'darkness of vision'. I tried to make sense of it at first but that is literally what they meant. I had seen the young and the old with it. It was seen across the whole age range. They all said the same, that it usually came suddenly. It occurred to me this too could be curse related. I couldn't medically test it but, in every person whom I prayed for and broke off the curse followed by a blessing on their eyes, they *all* were able to see with normal vision again. It was as simple as that with one hundred percent healed.

I discovered that 'dark vision' was actually mentioned in the book of Psalms and Paul referred to this same passage in Romans. It says, *'May their eyes be darkened and backs bent forever'* (Psalm 69:23, Romans 11:10). This was a curse being spoken over David's enemies. Dark vision was the result of a curse.

Paul saw how a sorcerer named Elymas was opposing God by trying to stop the proconsul from hearing the word of God. It says in Acts, after Paul and Barnabus had been sent to Cyprus, *'Now when they had gone through the island to Paphos, they found a certain sorcerer, a false prophet, a Jew whose name was Bar-Jesus, who was with the proconsul, Sergius Paulus, an intelligent man.*

*This man called for Barnabus and Saul and sought to hear the word of God. **But Elymas the sorcerer, withstood them, seeking to turn the proconsul away from the faith. Then Saul, who also is called Paul, filled with the Holy Spirit, looked intently at him and said, "Oh full of all deceit and all fraud, you son of the devil, you enemy of all righteousness, will you not cease perverting the straight ways of the Lord? And now indeed, the hand of the Lord is upon you, and you shall be blind, not seeing the sun for a time". And immediately a dark mist fell on him and he went around seeking someone to lead him by the hand.** Then the proconsul believed, when he saw what had been done, being astonished at the teaching of the Lord'* (Acts 13:6-12). Here, Paul was demonstrating to the proconsul that the power of God was greater than the power of the sorcerer and this sorcerer was going to experience dark vision or the inability to see for a period of time as a result of his sins.

Prior to his conversion, Saul could see nothing after his encounter on the road to Damascus with Jesus. Here it was after seeing the glory of God, he fell blind for three days until God sent another disciple, Ananias, to lay hands on him so he could see again. It says after Ananias placed his hands on Saul *'something like scales fell from Saul's eyes and he could see again '*(Acts 9:8-18).

Jesus Strengthens the Weary

There were occasions when I and others in the medical team would feel exhausted, either with lack of sleep, the heat or simply tired from going from village to village. Once, when we were feeling quite exhausted and about to start a clinic, we asked God to give us His strength. Shortly after, we were all feeling alert and actually finished feeling more energised than when we started. However, there was one occasion when the team had to return a fair distance for their lunch break. The half that decided to go back for some lunch didn't return due to lethargy and not wanting to walk back in the midday heat. The half that carried on with me finished feeling energised as well as the receiving the reward of witnessing the many healings that took place.

If we relied on our feelings, we would never do anything! The enemy can throw lethargy at us, especially when we are stepping into God's will, be it in prayer meetings, preaching, running healing clinics or whatever we may do for God. We need to discern this and let our spirit rise above our flesh as we step out by faith. Then the tiredness will lift and God will equip us by the power of His Spirit to do that which He has called us to do!

Opposition on Outreach

Whenever we step out onto enemy territory to do Kingdom work, we can expect to face some opposition. The enemy doesn't like us coming into his camp so he attempts to stop us through inflicting sickness, fear, apathy, disunity, conflict, negative thoughts or using other means to keep us out. The enemy threw a storm at Jesus and His disciples to try and stop them getting across the lake to set the demon-possessed man free (Mark 4:35-5:8). We need to recognise this and see it for what it really is.

On one occasion, I had diarrhoea the morning we were due to leave for an outreach. I knew in my heart God wanted me to go for He was going to do much in that village. I rebuked the sickness and, in faith, got in the car and went on outreach. God was faithful back and the symptoms instantly disappeared as I obeyed and went.

There have also been times when the enemy has thrown insult or criticism my way just before setting off on outreach. I have had to not react to this or open my heart to negative thoughts or speech and keep all doors of my heart closed to the enemy.

It's important to seek knowledge and revelation from God before entering new villages to see if there are any curses or spiritual strongholds over the village. If so, then they need to be dealt with as led by the Holy Spirit in prayer. God gives us His authority when He wants us to overcome enemy strongholds. It is important we do it all through the work of His Spirit in us and not through our own flesh. We can claim back the ground by prayer-walking around it and inviting God's Kingdom to come and reign in the village. Sadly, many people live in fear of being cursed or go themselves to witchdoctors so they can put curses on their enemies. God wants to raise up His people to worship Him in spirit and in truth, being in awe of His power instead of fearing Satan's power.

Another time we had travelled seven hours on road and dirt track to reach a village. We were told initially we were not welcomed because they thought what we had was probably poison and going to harm the people 'like the mosquito nets did'. I later found out that previous white people had given them some mosquito nets that had been chemically treated and had caused an irritation to their skin. This had caused them to fear white man's medicine.

That night a group of us did nothing but intercede for the village and prayed God's Kingdom come and will be done. We broke off any lies of the enemy and spoke peace to the village and an open heaven over the area. We then went to sleep.

The next morning, Eric and I met up with the two chiefs, who were of another faith, along with the whole village. To our surprise, the two chiefs said they realised that we had come a long way and were touched we would do this. As a result, they told the people they had their permission to come to the clinic. Not only that, they then said they didn't mind if the people accepted Jesus into their lives! Eric and I looked at each other in utter amazement, completely stunned by what we heard. Sure enough, one hundred percent of the people we saw in clinic that day said yes to accepting Jesus in their hearts and receiving prayer for healing. We both knew this was the result of the prayer the night before. We had breakthrough! What a mighty God we were serving!

Septic Arthritis Healed

One of the teenage Iris children came to the clinic with a five day history of a swollen, painful knee. It was twice the size of her other knee. On examination it looked like it could be septic arthritis. It was confirmed when I withdrew at least twenty millilitres of exudate or pus from her knee joint. Back in England she would have received intravenous antibiotics and had expert care in her management; but she didn't want another needle in her joint and we had no intravenous antibiotics at the time to give her. We gave her the best oral antibiotic we had available and prayed with her. I was concerned she may develop a fixed flexion contracture or restricted knee movement from the infection, but she adamantly refused to go into hospital even for private treatment. Since she was Gillick competent (that is, mentally competent and of age to make her own decisions), we couldn't force her against her own will. However, she had faith in her Heavenly Father and adamantly told us He would heal her! Her swelling miraculously went down each day. After three days, she was almost fully weight bearing on her swollen leg. By seven days, she was totally healed! This was truly a miracle! I was greatly humbled. God took what little I could offer and He did the rest. He deserved all the glory, for there were no complications whatsoever and the recovery was quick. God loves it when we give Him our meagre offering, especially when it is all we have for He will bless it and provide the rest that is needed!

Unconscious Student

There was an African Bible school student who had been found unconscious in his bed and I was called to see him. On examination, his eyes were closed and he didn't respond to my voice or any pain as I pressed firmly on his sternum. As I examined his eyes, they rolled to the sides and he was unable to look straight at me. But when another person talked to him, I saw his eyes open briefly and saw a movement of his arms. This was an unusual response for someone that was supposedly in an unconscious state so I realised we were probably dealing with something spiritual. The people around were panicking and urging me to get him to the hospital, but I wanted to pray for him first. As I commanded the spirit of infirmity and death to leave his body, he began to shake all over. Within a minute or so he stopped shaking, got up fully conscious and asked for a drink of water. It turned out he was a new student. Unfortunately, it's not uncommon for new students to be cursed by their local people when news gets around that they are leaving their village and families (including home responsibilities) to attend a Bible school, especially in a non-Christian country.

On another occasion, I was asked to go and see a visitor who was unconscious in her bed. As I went, the room was full of other visitors all highly concerned. There was a visiting doctor with me who was keen to do the emergency medical intervention for someone who was unconscious. After an initial examination noting her clinical observations were normal, I had a check in my spirit that there was something else going on. I realised the incidence happened when the room was full of onlookers. I asked all the visitors to step outside and the visiting doctor to hold back for a moment. We stopped giving attention to the person and just quietly observed. Within minutes, the person regained consciousness and was looking around to see who was there. No medical intervention was needed. It turned out after further questioning that the person had significant emotional and spiritual issues that needed to be dealt with. This was a non-organic case that didn't require medical intervention but rather inner healing.

In England, I have managed many unconscious children brought to the accident and emergency department, especially whilst working on the intensive care unit. My medical approach is based on the guidelines and training I have received in the UK. However, I believe it is still important to think of possible spiritual or emotional causes in the differential diagnosis so not to misdiagnose or give inappropriate medical care where not needed.

Chapter 6

EXTENDED OUTREACHES

'May the God who gives endurance and encouragement give you
a spirit of unity *among yourselves as you follow Christ Jesus'.*
(Romans 15:5)

Extended outreaches took place at the end of a mission school and would last around two weeks. We would usually drive to another province, stopping off at different villages and churches en route. On one occasion, I had the opportunity to take a team to another war-torn nation in Africa. Regardless of where we travelled, the principles remained the same.

Team Unity
One of the key things I learnt most during these outreaches was the importance of team building and unity. Getting on well with others is not the same as being united together in the Spirit. In order to come under the anointing and protection of the Holy Spirit, we need to be united together in His Spirit. This comes through praying and worshipping together. It may include participating in taking communion, or the washing of each other's feet. Corporate prayer, including praying for one another, is an important key for team unity. We must invest our time in this if we desire to work in the unity of the Spirit and under His anointing. I also believe that team unity is vital if we do not want to come under the attack of the enemy.

Did you know God is more interested in a united team than He is about how many people get saved or healed? It's true! I saw Him do this on our extended outreaches. If a team hadn't sorted out their personal issues before setting out together, then

God would deal with them on the outreach. It matters more to God that a team represents His character and Kingdom values (like honour, generosity, humility, love and unity) than it does by what they achieve. This is why God usually has to deal with our personal issues in private before He releases us to work for Him in public. Otherwise, it could get rather messy and we could end up putting people off from entering His Kingdom. We may have our own agenda and what we want to achieve, but is this in line with God's agenda? We need to let Him deal with all that needs sorting out in us first, before we try and sort others out. It is good to get rid of any bad fruit that others may see and instead display His Kingdom fruit in all we say and do.

Some of the common issues we had to deal with in our teams included selfishness, criticism, gossip, disunity and complaining. We are usually critical towards others when they don't meet up to our standards or expectations. God challenged me on this when He asked me if I ever met up to His standards or expectations. I had to humbly laugh when I realised not. Yet, He still loves me unconditionally and still encourages me when I make mistakes. Expectation can breed disappointment when people don't live up to it. I believe we should try to see others through the eyes of God and offer encouragement by cheering them on, instead of judging them when they fail our expectations.

As we gathered together for prayer and worship, God in His love and mercy, exposed these areas. The team members then willingly repented and sought forgiveness from God and one another. We then had a beautiful time of washing each other's dirty feet and feeling the power and Presence of His Spirit move among us. At one point, God challenged individuals to give away what treats they had brought for themselves to other members in the team. It was a powerful time and released a true sense of love and unity.

Psalm 133 says: '*How good and pleasant it is when brothers live together in unity! It is like precious oil poured on the head... for there the Lord bestows His blessing*'. His anointing is released where there is unity in the Spirit. As God's children, we are also called to clothe ourselves with compassion, kindness, humility, gentleness and patience. We are to bear with one another and forgive what grievances we may have against each other (Colossians 3:12-14). Paul knew the powerful effect of true unity and continually encouraged it amongst all believers, including speaking the truth in love (Ephesians 4:15).

God did amazing things with each team as we remained united in the Spirit. The Spirit was able to flow in power among us and, as a result of spiritually getting the team ready the weeks beforehand, we were able to accomplish so much more in the Kingdom for Him.

Reaching Out Just for the One

I must admit I was feeling a bit disappointed when we had visited a village but only managed to reach out to one family. I wanted the clinic to be open to everyone in this village and not just this family of fifteen or so people. Then I was reminded of Jesus' visit to the well and His encounter with the one Samaritan woman. Jesus reached out to this one lady and she then reached out to the rest of her village. I knew I had to trust God's hand in this matter. Sometimes it may be just the one person or family whom we reach out to that may do amazing things in God's Kingdom.

Are we willing to travel far to reach out for just the one person? It says in Zechariah 4:10 that we are not to despise the day of small things! If we can't do the small things God asks us to do, then He will not trust us with the big things.

Consecrating Land

At a later date, the opportunity came to go on another extended outreach. We had the choice of two. On one of the outreaches there would be plenty of opportunities to do clinic work but on the other there would be little. I kept feeling in my spirit that we were to do the outreach which had little opportunity for clinic work. This was a case where I had to overcome my rational thinking and logic with what God's Spirit was saying. The wisdom revealed to us by God's Spirit may appear foolish to man but God's thoughts are not our thoughts neither are our ways His (1 Corinthians 2:6-16, Isaiah 55:8).

We were obedient to His Spirit and chose the outreach with little clinic opportunity. On this outreach, one of the places where we stayed was on a plot of newly bought land which was for the further use of Iris Ministries. On our first night, we encountered sting insects, scorpions, spiders and other vile things like I have never experienced before. They were all over our tents. We even saw huge spiders, not knowing if they were venomous or not. One member in the team was bitten by a scorpion on her hand when she opened up her tent. We prayed for her and the pain gradually left. It really felt like we were plagued with infesting creatures and it was as if they represented black spiritual blobs over the land.

The next day we decided to pray over the land and consecrate it. First, God gave a vision of the team, along with the local pastors, walking in a line around the periphery of the land. In the Spirit I saw the land being set on fire and then God consuming the whole land with His holy fire. To do this, we chose to pour consecrated water around the borders. There just happened to be four empty water bottles and clean rain water which had collected in a puddle on top of a huge tent. We were able to fill all four bottles with the rain water. I felt this represented water from Heaven, which had not yet reached the ground. We prayed over the water and asked God to bless it. The four bottles were for the four borders. Just as we were about to start, the sky looked grey throughout and, sure enough, it started to rain. We prayed and asked God to hold the clouds back and shine His light down as we walked around the land. Within minutes, it stopped and blue sky appeared. The team, along with the local pastors, started worshipping and praying aloud as we marched around the land, pouring the consecrated water along its borders. Just as we finished, it started to rain again!

A few days later we ended up spending another night at this base, but this time noticed that the ground was clean. Nobody saw any spiders, sting insects or scorpions. Our tents also remained clean! I believe after we did this prophetic act under the leading of the Holy Spirit, God did something in the supernatural. This land had now been consecrated for further Kingdom use.

Outreach to a War-torn Nation

In 2008, I went with a team to a base that was being established in a war-torn nation. This was a nation which was still at war with itself, where the government in the North was fighting the people groups in the South. It was the norm to hear gunshots in the night or landmines go off as well as seeing people with blown off limbs walking with crutches in the street. Hence, it was important that we went as a team not only united in the Spirit, but also yielded to the will of God instead of our own fancy agendas. So we invested time together for the four weeks before we were due to depart. In this time we worshipped, prayed, took communion and washed each other's feet. We dealt with any issues that God brought to our attention, so they wouldn't become stumbling blocks while we were out there. We wanted to be ready and available for whatever He wanted us to do for Him. This was going to be a different outreach for sure.

When we arrived at the base, there was a small child who had a fever and was lying on the floor, unable to play with the other children. I didn't have the resources to do medical tests so I simply laid my hand on his burning forehead and rebuked the fever. Less than half an hour later, the fever was gone and the child was playing with the other children. This reminded me of when Jesus rebuked the fever and it left Peter's mother-in-law and she got up and continued as normal (Mathew 8:14-15).

On one outreach we went with a lorry load of older children from the Iris base to a village nearby. This time we laid hands on the Iris children so that they could go and pray for the sick. It was lovely seeing them praying in pairs for people in this village and God healing the sick through them.

Supernatural Mango

The team met up to pray before visiting a church near the border. As we were finishing our time of prayer, a yellow mango suddenly fell right in our midst from a tree nearby. One of the African members of staff picked it up and went away, only to bring it back to us, nicely cut into chunks. It was the most delicious mango fruit I had ever tasted and everyone else thought the same. When I mentioned this to the Iris leader, she laughed and said it was not mango season and wondered if I had realised this. I took a closer look and, sure enough, the mango trees were in flower. It would be another few months before the fruit was due. We had received a supernatural, yellow mango! That was why it tasted so delicious - it was from Heaven itself! I was in awe of this and marvelled at what I had witnessed take place. A pastor commented it was the *first fruit* that God had given us. It was the beginning of much spiritual fruit that was to be harvested in this nation.

One thing I have realised is how faithful God is to those who are willing to step out for Him. He always rewards His fellow servants especially when it has cost them something to say yes to His call. His light shines even brighter in the dark nations. And it is when we are dependent on Him for everything, having stepped out in faith, that we see more of His glorious power at work and observe supernatural things happening around us as if it were all normal.

Chapter 7

ISLAND OUTREACHES

*'He **had compassion** on them and **healed their sick'**.*
(Mathew 14:14)

I once had a dream of being picked up in a small four seated plane and flying off to remote islands. This was followed by a vision of surfing on the waves to the different islands but without any surf board, just my bare feet on the waves. I had forgotten about the dream until I met a pilot, named Joe, who had just joined the mission staff. The first time we met, we both knew it was a God appointment and we would be doing medical missions of some sort together in the future. Then an opportunity came. *What about reaching out to some of the islands with medical aid?*

Apparently on each of the inhabited islands, 99% of the people were of other faiths and 1% were Christians. After Joe was able to make contact with leaders on two of the islands, the medical team got ready to go but this time it would be a much smaller team. Joe could only take four passengers in his plane and, since the tribes on the islands spoke a different language, we needed two translators to come and assist us. After getting the necessary approval and government signed documentation, we showed it to the medical officers and chiefs on each island who then gave us the permission to set up a clinic.

Different Strategy to Reach Out to Other Faiths
God revealed to me that He had a different strategy for the people on the islands. We were to offer them healing like it was a gift wrapped up for them. We were not to initially approach them by telling them about Jesus or leading them in repentant prayer, but

to simply reveal His love to them. They had to do nothing but say yes to our love offering. The island ministry would be different in that I could see we were to make regular contact with the people, so they could get to know and trust us. It was going to be through our friendship and love that they would come to Jesus.

I was reminded of Paul when he spoke to the Gentile people. He chose his words and didn't mention Jesus' Name when telling them about God (Acts 17:22-31). Likewise, I was to be sensitive to this and mention only God's name (since they were familiar with God) and let Him do the rest. As we gradually got to build a relationship with them on the different visits, then we could share more of God's love and tell them about His Son, Jesus.

First Island

It was another adventure with God. On our first island outreach, we saw a full 180 degree rainbow as we flew across the ocean. It was a spectacular view while in the air. We had a bumpy land as the small plane came down on an uneven grass landing strip that looked like it hadn't been used in a long time. Then we found a sheltered spot under some coconut palm trees where we could set up the clinic. It was absolutely sweltering and we desperately needed some breeze. With the sweat that was pouring off our bodies, we could hardly drink enough water to stay hydrated.

Word soon got around on this three mile long island that we were there. Not all of the 4000 inhabitants were around for many were out fishing. However, the sick were still around and able to come to the clinic. If they were unable to come then we would visit them in their mud huts.

One old lady came to the clinic with a walking stick. Her hunched back was bent double and her eyes stared towards the ground. She was unable to look up and appeared depressed as she asked for medicines for her chronic body aches. I felt led to ask her if she believed in God and she said yes. I asked if she believed He could heal her and again she replied yes. I then asked her if I could pray for her. She thought, 'Why not?' and agreed.

God had taught me previously that He can set people free and heal them through a gentle voice, for it's about His authority in us and not the loudness of our voices. So I carefully chose my words and, with a gentle voice, asked God to remove her pain and anything 'not of Him'. I also asked Him to reveal His love to her. As I placed my hand on her back, I felt heat in my hand and knew her back was being healed. I asked her how she was and to test her body. She was able to fully extend her back and could now look up as if she never had a problem. She still had some aches in her lower leg, but I didn't want to push it too much on our first visit. Instead, I gave her some analgesia for that. She left with her back upright and face looking up, but sadly no smile. The moment she stood outside the tent there was an uproar and clapping of hands by the women who were still waiting to be seen, for they were utterly amazed to see her healed and walking outside with a normal posture.

We came back to the same island a week later to build up trust with the people. I saw the same old lady again as she walked into the tent with her back once again bent double, exactly the same as it was before. I asked her what happened. She said that she had been fine all week until her daughter did something to upset her and she got angry. The moment she responded in anger (and whatever other negative attitudes she displayed), her back bent double to the same as it was before. This explained what had happened. I asked her if she had other people that she felt bitter and angry towards. Many! But she was not willing to forgive any. I explained that if she forgave, God would heal her completely. She sadly refused and just wanted the medication. I couldn't believe that it was more important for her to harbour such anger, bitterness and unforgiveness than it was to have her back healed. This made me see just how much love and mercy God had given her the first time around when He was willing to heal her back without her even repenting of sins or forgiving others. I was in awe of God's mercy for this woman, but also saddened by her decision not to forgive.

It is also true to say that if we haven't dealt with the root cause of a sickness or disease, then the symptoms will manifest again in the future when the individual performs the same sin. The fruit is a manifestation of the root! This ladies double bent back was a manifestation of her bitterness and unforgiveness. This reminded me of the bent over lady in the Bible who had been *crippled by a spirit* for eighteen years. Jesus healed her by setting her free from the *spirit of infirmity* (Luke 13:10-13). Likewise, when Jesus healed the crippled man and bumped into him again He told him to *sin no more* or he would be worse off (John 5:14). This is an important lesson that in order to *stay healed*, we are to *sin no more* or not give opportunity to the enemy to come and inflict sickness on us. Paul says, *'In your anger do not sin...and do not give the devil a foothold'* (Ephesians 4:26-28).

When we re-visited this island a few months later we were asked why we hadn't returned sooner. The truth was that we had started doing mobile clinics on some of the other islands, so we alternated the weekends that were available to do either an island outreach or an inland outreach. On this visit, there happened to be a wedding taking place and the chief told the guests who had come from neighbouring islands that they were welcome to go to the free clinic.

We saw a lady who was a teacher from another island who had chronic pain down her leg. She believed God could heal and let us pray for her. She tested her leg and it was completely healed! She had never experienced God's healing power before and I encouraged her to teach this to her pupils.

I sensed there was a change in the atmosphere on this island, in that the people were now more welcoming and friendly and less sceptical or fearful of us. A trust was developing and they were seeing that we were truly there to help them and not harm them in any way. As we left, we were asked when were we going to come back and were even given some fresh coconuts straight from their trees. A member of the team commented it was as if something had been planted in the dry ground and was now taking root and growth, though still at the early stages. I couldn't have agreed more.

Second Island

The people on the second island appeared more welcoming and very open to prayer. Here we pitched our tent at a focal point on the island. It was next to their bore-hole well, so people could get their natural water but also come and drink of His living waters in the clinic tent.

One old lady crawled on her hands and knees into the tent. She had severely bowed legs and was unable to walk. She was also severely crippled with what looked like swollen arthritic knees and hips. She looked miserable and was in considerable pain. It turned out she had suffered with reduced mobility for many years. When questioned, she had no problem believing that God could heal her and was keen to receive prayer. After prayer I asked her to try and stand up. She screwed up her face as she expressed immense pain, but she still attempted to get up and walk. I even wondered if I should be asking her to do this when I saw the agony she was going through, but something in me said *believe*. I then imagined her in my mind dancing before the Lord and declared that she would be able to dance with full use of her legs in Jesus' Name. Within about thirty seconds, her facial expression started to change from a face expressing absolute agony to a more serene looking face with a beautiful smile. It was wonderful to watch. She not only danced on the spot with me but she also jogged home, still with her bowed legs, turning around and waving to me with a beaming smile on her face. I was stunned and stood watching until she was out of view.

We saw the same woman again a few months later with an unhappy look on her face. Her legs weren't the problem; she was still pain free and very mobile. However, since our last visit she suddenly started having what seemed like fits. She described going dizzy and falling to the floor, with a loss of consciousness at least five or more times a day. I thought this was rather odd, especially since the timing was after God had healed her of her arthritic joints and she had accepted Jesus in her life. Knowing there was witchcraft on the island and how the enemy likes to throw things at God's children, we broke off any witchcraft, including curses, in Jesus' Name and commanded any epileptic spirit to go. I then informed her that if she felt a funny episode coming on, she had authority to tell it to go in Jesus' Name. She was still unhappy for she was hoping to get some medicine. Hours later, she came back. She said she felt another funny episode coming on but this time she rebuked it in Jesus' Name, demonstrating so with her pointed finger. As she did, it immediately stopped. Praise God! She had learned how to be healed by simply rebuking the attacks, for she now had God's Spirit and authority in her to do this. One sad face was now smiling again for she had seen God's Spirit at work in her. She said she wanted to go around the whole island praying for others to be healed too. It was a special moment seeing an old lady becoming young in her spirit, with both the passion and faith to heal the sick on her island because of what God had done in her life. As she had freely received, so she was willing to freely give.

Another lady I saw complained of something moving in her body causing fire in her arms and pain in her back and head. She agreed it was probably spiritual and repented of going to the witchdoctor. After prayer, she felt a sweat come on her and said she felt something leave her body. She was now pain free.

A different woman then came into the tent with what she described as cloudy vision and itchy eyes. She had been many times to the witchdoctor but was no better. She said her own prayer of repentance and invited Jesus to heal her. As I prayed, I felt led to pour water (which had already been prayed over and blessed by God) on her eyes. She blinked and blinked again then shook her head thanking Jesus for healing her. She said a heaviness lifted from her eyes and she now could see normally again. This was similar to the others who were healed of their dark vision.

On this island the people were much more open to prayer. It felt a safe place to discuss about the effects of witchcraft on the body and educate the people about the source of their symptoms while revealing that God could heal and set them free. I felt I could be more open with them on subsequent visits as they began to trust us.

Word spread like wild fire of the healings taking place. This was good and exciting news that made people open to receive prayer at the clinic for they had either heard testimonies or were witnesses themselves to God's healing power. On the fifth visit I witnessed a spiritual breakthrough. At least fifteen of the women I saw accepted Jesus into their lives and, those who refused, still wanted prayer for healing. When I asked them why they wanted prayer but not Jesus, they said 'because it is good and works'.

Third Island

There was eventually opportunity to visit a third island. On our way there for the first time, we hit a band of thick dark clouds and were going to have to go through a thunderstorm. Joe tried his best to go around it so to avoid it, but we were going to still encounter it. I prayed silently, trusting God's big hand would protect the little plane. I felt very small indeed, aware that a bolt of lightning was more likely to contact the plane before hitting the ocean. We did, however, come out of it into glorious light and were able to make a safe landing.

We met a different group of people and they too were open for prayer. We saw God touch their bodies and heal them of body pain or weaknesses. On this island a local health worker assisted us in the clinic, but he was reluctant to translate for us when we prayed for the people. In spite of his attitude, the people themselves were hungry for prayer and God reached out and healed them. He became appreciative when we treated his sick children and asked if we could also pray for them. We happily obliged.

Once again, we saw many healed of 'dark vision' and body aches. One lady was dancing on the spot as she tested out her pain free body. Another lady had earache. After prayer, she smiled and said something *left her ear* and she had no more pain. I believe she was referring to a demonic spirit that was behind her symptom.

Different Islands, Different People

It's important to realise that God deals with different people in different nations in different ways. We need to follow Him and do as He shows us what to do, for He will have a different strategy each time we reach out to a different group of people. He knows them best and knows the best approach to woo them with His love into His Kingdom. Then there will be success instead of opposition or disappointment. We need to be led by His Spirit and approach His people as He desires, so we have minimal flaws but optimum outcome.

Jesus healed people with similar ailments differently. This was seen when He healed five blind men. Jesus healed the man who was born blind by spitting on the ground first, then making mud with the saliva, followed by putting it on the man's eyes. Finally, He told the man to go and wash his eyes in a pool (John 9:6). However, the blind beggar who cried out to Jesus received instant healing. Jesus replied, 'Receive your sight; your faith has healed you', and he was immediately healed (Luke 18:35-43). The blind man at Bethsaida was healed after Jesus spat on the man's eyes and put His hands on them, but this actually took two attempts (Mark 8:22-26). The two blind men who were sitting by the roadside when they heard Jesus was passing by cried out for Him to heal their sight. Jesus had compassion on them and touched their eyes and they were immediately healed (Mathew 20:29-34).

Jesus healed these five blind men differently, according to what the Holy Spirit revealed to Him concerning each individual. Hence, we are to do as the Holy Spirit reveals and approach each person the way He wants us to. We must not use formulas or try and replicate what may have worked elsewhere, but do as He shows us to. He is omnipotent and omniscient and we are simply His servants through whom He chooses to do His mighty works.

Chapter 8

HEALING & DELIVERANCE (I)

HOW DID JESUS AND HIS DISCIPLES HEAL THE SICK?

*'I tell you the truth, anyone who has faith in Me will do what I have
been doing. He will do even greater things than these because
I am going to the Father'.
(John 4:12)*

Luke was a doctor and a Gentile (Colossians 3:14). He testifies in both the Gospel of Luke and book of Acts to the amazing healings that took place with Jesus and His disciples. *'When Jesus had called the twelve disciples together,* **He gave them power** *and* **authority** *to* **drive out demons** *and to* **cure diseases** *and He sent them out to* **preach the Kingdom of God** *and* **to heal the sick'** (Luke 9:1-2). The Greek word for salvation is *'sozo'*. Salvation here doesn't just mean being saved; it also refers to being healed and set free from any spiritual bondage. Jesus sent His disciples not just to preach the Kingdom but to also heal the sick and drive out demons!

Salvation is for all, for it says that God sent His one and only Son that *whoever* believes in Him will not perish but have eternal life (John 3:16). However, the Greek word *'sozo'* that was used in the Gospels was used many times in the context of healing or being made whole. We see that the word sozo refers to being 'saved' in Luke 19:10: *'For the Son of Man came to seek and to save (sozo) what was lost'*. However, sozo refers to being 'healed' in Mathew 9:22: *'Take heart daughter, your faith has healed (sozo) you'*. Likewise, sozo refers to being delivered and made well in Luke 8:36: *'The demon possessed man had been cured (sozo)'*. Just as it is

85

God's will for all to be saved, so it is also God's will for *all* to be healed and set free.

I believe we are missing a fundamental part to evangelism if we only preach about the Kingdom without demonstrating His power and love through signs and wonders, including healing and deliverance. Likewise, we are missing a major part of healing if we don't include salvation and deliverance where it is needed. This is what Jesus taught me on the job as I went in the different villages and learnt from Him how to treat the sick. I wanted to reach out to the sick but, for the majority, this meant I had to first invite them into God's Kingdom to know Jesus, and then set them free from witchcraft and any demonic bondage that was stopping them from being healed.

I had considered doing some training on deliverance ministry before going to Africa, but this wasn't God's will for me. Instead I was to learn on the job, just like He taught His disciples. We learn by doing.

Jesus encouraged His disciples to learn by doing, even though they were new at the job and made many mistakes. He taught them through their mistakes and at times this even included rebuking them. When Jesus and His disciples were not welcomed in a Samaritan village, His disciples James and John commented, '"*Lord, do You want us to call fire down from Heaven and destroy them?" But Jesus turned and rebuked them and they went to another village*' (Luke 9:51-56). Even when we make mistakes or don't say the right things, God is sovereign and can heal anyone, at any time, however He chooses.

This reminds me of a time when I was with Youth With A Mission (YWAM) doing my Discipleship Training School in my gap year before medical school. I met an eighteen year old boy who had been dabbling in white witchcraft. We connected when we found we had something in common in that our fathers were both Anglican priests. The young man tried to convince me that white witchcraft was a good thing and not bad. God's Spirit came on me as I told him he had to choose between the two kingdoms, God's or Satan's. There was a split moment when he came under the conviction of the Holy Spirit and agreed for me to pray for him there and then. At that time there was no one else free to pray with me. Every leader was already engaged in praying for someone else and instead I was encouraged to go and pray for him on my own. I didn't really know what to pray, so I said a very short prayer. For the next five minutes I witnessed him have a supernatural encounter with Jesus as he remained still, in silence, with his eyes closed. Later he said he saw a black cloak fall from his body and then a brilliant white light shining in front of him. I asked him what this light was and he said, 'Jesus'. His radiant face testified to his encounter. I was amazed at what had happened. God reminded me how inexperienced I was when I prayed for this teenager; yet He could still work through me and simply delighted in my willingness to be His vessel.

In this encounter, it was Jesus who did the work, not me. This is what Jesus said to His disciples when He reminded them that without Him abiding in them they could do nothing (John 15:5). Yes, we can achieve many things in our own strength and natural abilities, but when it comes to living a life as a servant and disciple of the Lord, we can only heal the sick, raise the dead and set the captives free through the power of His Spirit flowing in and through us. We mustn't forget that God also sends His ministering warrior angels who are each on specific assignments to save, deliver, heal the sick and minister specifically to the needs of every person we pray for. *'Are not all angels ministering spirits sent to serve those who will inherit salvation?'* (Hebrews 1:14).

Salvation is more than being saved. Salvation refers to our spiritual journey with God. Being saved is at the start of this journey. Hence, salvation is often referred to in the present and ongoing tense as well as future tense. Paul says we are to work out our salvation with fear and trembling (Philippians 2:12). It became the norm for me to see people get healed and set free when they accepted Jesus into their lives.

God doesn't need us to do His work, but He chooses us to co-labour with Him. He made it clear to me that He didn't need my skills and medical expertise to work alongside Him. He was looking for someone who was simply willing to surrender all they had to follow Him and do what He was doing.

Jesus said He could do nothing by Himself but only what He saw His Father doing (John 5:19, Mathew 7:21). We must never forget that it is not us who does the healing but it is the work of the Holy Spirit! God is the one who heals and we can simply be His vessels to release His healing power through His Holy Spirit at work in and through us! The question is: *Are we willing to be His servant vessels where we can be His hands, His eyes and His mouth to the unreached, sick and hurting people in the world?*

HOW DID JESUS HEAL THE SICK?

'Jesus went throughout Galilee, teaching in their synagogues, preaching the Good News of the Kingdom and **healing every sickness and disease** *among the people... people brought to Him* **all who were ill** *with* **various diseases**, *those* **suffering with severe pain, the demon-possessed**, *those* **having seizures**, *and* **the paralyzed, and He healed them'** (Mathew 4:23-24).

There was no sickness or disease that Jesus couldn't heal. He healed ALL who were brought to Him. It ranged from physical to emotional to spiritual, if not all in one go. Many times they were healed physically after He spoke forgiveness over them or bound up a demon and commanded it to leave them. This side of medicine and healing is sadly neglected in the medical profession, partly because it is little understood and scientists are looking for organic proof to sickness and disease instead of looking into the power and effect of forgiveness and freedom from demonic bondage on the body. So let's look at the spiritual tools Jesus used to heal the sick.

1) Prayer & Fasting

Before Jesus stepped into His ministry, He had His faith tested and underwent many trials, especially during His forty days of prayer and fasting. At times, when Jesus let His disciples experiment on healing the sick, they failed miserably. On one occasion they were unable to cast a spirit out of a boy who was fitting. Jesus told them that it was their lack of faith that caused this not to happen. In some translations Jesus said this evil spirit would only come out with prayer *and fasting* (Mathew 17:19-21). Fasting is a whole subject in itself, but it is essentially a discipline where our flesh submits to our spirit and God can empower us as we focus more on Him by yielding ourselves to Him.

I believe greater spiritual authority is released in us when we fast from our flesh and things of this world, focusing instead on His Spirit. Don't forget that Satanists even fast for 'spiritual breakthrough' to bring division, destruction and even death in people's lives. If they can cause breakthrough and release of demonic power through fasting, think how powerful it is when Christians fast and God releases His warrior angels, just like when Daniel prayed and fasted to bring Kingdom breakthrough (Daniel 10:2-14).

Jesus taught His disciples to pray, *'Your Kingdom come, Your will be done, on earth as it is in Heaven'* (Mathew 6:10). We are to call His Kingdom and will forth on earth as we see it is taking place in Heaven. This is a major part of breakthrough prayer.

2) *Anointing & Power*

The time in the wilderness was actually a season of preparation for Jesus. As mentioned previously, Jesus entered the desert **'filled with the Holy Spirit'**, but He returned to Galilee *'in the power of the Spirit'* (Luke 4:14). It was then that He entered His full time ministry. Peter says how God **anointed** Jesus with the **Holy Spirit and power** and how He went around doing good, healing all who were under the power of the devil, *because God was with Him* (Acts 10:38).

Jesus fulfilled what was written in Isaiah 61:1, *'The Spirit of the Lord is on Me, because the Lord has anointed Me...'* The Spirit of God that rested upon Jesus anointed Him to minister to the sick. This same Spirit that rested upon Jesus also gave Him the Spirit of wisdom, understanding, knowledge, counsel, power and the fear of the Lord. *'A shoot will come up from Jesse; from his roots a Branch will bear fruit. The Spirit of the Lord will rest on Him - the Spirit of wisdom and of understanding, the Spirit of counsel and of power, the Spirit of knowledge and of the fear of the Lord - and He will delight in the fear of the Lord'* (Isaiah 11:1-3).

If we carry God's anointing and Presence, then no demon, principality or even Satan himself, shall we fear. We will be able to fearlessly confront whatever we face, when we choose to delight in the fear of the Lord and stand in the presence of an awesome God.

Being filled with the Holy Spirit is for ourselves, whereas being anointed under the power of the Spirit is for the work God has called us to. As we overcome the challenges and opposition in our life and desire more intimacy with God, He releases more of His authority and power on us. He anoints us to step into the ministry He has called us to serve Him in, but this is in His timing when He sees we are ready (not when we think we are or not).

Luke comments, *'Those troubled by evil spirits were cured and the people all tried to touch Him, because **power was coming from Him** and **healing them all***' (Luke 6:19). Some Christians actually fear touching someone who either has a demon or contagious illness (like leprosy), for fear they will get it too. We have the power of Jesus in us! So we do not need to fear that we will receive what the sick person has. Those carrying the anointing to heal have greater power than the disease or demon they face or touch. He who is in us is greater than him in the world (1 John 4:4).

3) *Authority*

Jesus had authority over any sickness or demonic spirit simply because He was the Son of Man. His authority came from an intimate relationship with His Father and Jesus always submitted to the will of His Father (John 5:19-27). Jesus demonstrated His authority to the paralytic man by saying, *'So that you may know that the Son of Man has authority on earth to forgive sins.... get up, take your mat and go home'*, and the man did likewise (Mathew 9:6). His authority was also seen when He commanded the sickness or demon(s) to go and people were healed. What He spoke took place for there was authority in His words (Mathew 7:29). The sickness or demons had to submit to His authority.

Having authority over sickness and demons is what matters, and not the number of words spoken. Jesus didn't pray long prayers when healing the sick. He actually spoke directly at the sickness or demon(s) with very few words. He *'rebuked the fever'* and it left (Luke 4:39). He commanded the demon to *'Be quiet!'* then *'Get out!'* (Mark 1:25). To the demon-possessed, He drove out the evil spirits with just *a word* and healed the sick (Mathew 8:17). To the leper, He commanded, *'Be clean!'* (Mark

90

1:41). When raising Lazarus from the dead, He spoke with authority, *'Lazarus, come forth!'* (John 11:43). To the man born blind, He commanded him to, *'Go, wash in the pool of Siloam!'* and as he did, he was healed (John 9:7). When He was asked to heal a man who was both deaf and mute, He commanded, *'Be opened!'* (Mark 7:34).

When evil spirits saw Jesus, they would fall down in submission to Him, for they knew He had authority over them. *'For He had healed many, so that those with diseases were pushing forward to touch Him. Whenever the **evil spirits saw Him, they fell down before Him and cried out, "You are the Son of God".** But He gave them strict orders not to tell who He was'* (Mark 3:10-12). Likewise, when the man who was demon possessed with thousands of demons saw Jesus from a distance he ran, fell on his knees and the demons shouted, *'What do You want with me, Jesus, Son of the Most High God?'* (Mark 5:6). All demons were in fear of Jesus, for they knew who He was and that He had authority to cast them into hell. As Paul says, 'Every knee will bow in Heaven, on earth and under the earth and every tongue confess that Jesus Christ is Lord' (Philippians 2:10-11). *Amen.*

4) *Faith*

Jesus had *faith*. He knew and saw what His Father was doing and He followed His will all the time. Our faith should be such that we take action and do as we hear or see our Father doing in Heaven. Hope is like an arrow of prayer shot up to God without knowing God's response or will in the situation. Whereas faith is released when we have engaged our spirit with God and we can declare what we see Him doing, bringing it forth on earth as we see it taking place in Heaven. It is knowing what is on God's heart for man and agreeing in the Spirit even before we see it taking place in the natural realm on earth.

Faith was needed to heal the sick. It was either through the faith of Jesus or His disciples, the faith of a friend or family member, or the faith of the sick person themselves, where healing was released. Jesus told Jairus to *'just believe'* and his daughter would be healed (Luke 8:50). Jesus' reply to the centurion was, *'Go! It will be done just as you believed it would'*, and his servant was healed at that very hour (Mathew 8:13). Jesus said to the woman bleeding who touched His garment that *her faith* had healed her (Mathew 9:22, 14:36). He said the same to the blind man that according to his faith he would be healed (Mathew 9:27-30). However, Jesus healed few in His hometown due to their lack of faith (Mark 6:5-6). When the disciples asked Jesus why they failed to heal the fitting boy who had a deaf and mute spirit, Jesus said it was due to their lack of faith (Mathew 17:20). Likewise, when Jesus approached the demon-possessed man on the other side of the lake, His faith and authority were demonstrated as He spoke directly to the demons and commanded them to leave (Mark 5:1-17).

It is important to be with people of faith when praying for the sick and kindly asking those who are not of such faith to leave or wait outside. Even Jesus had to remove or ask those to leave who were full of doubt or carrying a spirit of mockery or mourning. When He went to see Jairus' daughter, He only took Peter, James and John in with Him as well as Jairus and his wife. He put everyone else outside (Mark 5:40). Likewise, when Jesus prayed for the blind man at Bethsaida, He took the blind man *and led him outside the village* and told him not to go back into that village. He had to do this so the man could receive healing. There may have been something taking place in the village or people carrying a negative influence or spirit that would have hindered or not allowed this healing to take place. Or it may have been that Jesus told him not to return for He didn't want attention or the crowds to follow Him (Mark 8:22-26). Whatever the reason was, we must understand that faith releases healing.

5) *Action & Laying on of Hands*
Healing was released many times through *stepping out* in faith. This is where action follows faith. Jesus told the paralytic to *get up, take up his mat and walk*. As he did, he was healed (Mark 2:11). It was after the blind man went and *washed his eyes in the pool* that he came back seeing (John 9:7). Jesus instructed the lepers to go and see the priests and *as they went,* they were healed (Luke 17:14). When healing a man who was both deaf and mute, Jesus put His *fingers in the man's ears* and then *spat and touched his*

tongue. After doing this He then looked up to Heaven and commanded, 'Be opened!' The man could then both hear and speak (Mark 7:33).

'*When the sun was setting, the people brought to Jesus all who had various kinds of sickness, and **laying His hands on each one**, He healed them*' (Luke 4:40). All whom Jesus laid His hands on were healed.

Note that Jesus had to pray more than once for a person on one occasion. He prayed and *laid hands twice* on a blind man's eyes before He could see with normal vision (Mark 8:25). Jesus spoke healing over the crippled woman *then He put His hands on her* and she immediately straightened her back (Luke 13:13).

Some Christians fear touching others who have contagious diseases or even demons for concern they'll get it too. This was also the mindset of the Israelites. The man with leprosy cried out on his knees, begging Jesus saying, '*Lord, if You are willing, You can make me clean*'. Jesus' reply was to first reach out and touch the man. Then He said, '*I am willing, be clean*' (Mark 1:40-41, Mathew 8:2-3). I believe Jesus touched the man first as a demonstration of His love and compassion to heal someone who was unclean. Jesus did not fear coming into physical contact with this contagious disease (or skin infested disease), for His power and authority were greater than the sickness or disease. Touch or the laying on of hands releases healing. Likewise, faith followed by action releases healing.

6) *Forgiveness of Sins*

Jesus demonstrated healing through the *forgiveness of sins*. He forgave the sins of the paralytic man who was lowered down on a mat to Him. He said, '*Son, your sins are forgiven*' (Mark 2:3-12). Then the man got up, took his mat and walked.

In another incidence, Jesus went up to a man who had been crippled for thirty-eight years and was lying by a pool. Jesus asked him, '*Do you want to get well?*' The man in a roundabout way said yes. So Jesus instructed him to '*Get up! Pick up your mat and walk*'. As he did, he was cured. Jesus later found him at the temple and told him to '*Stop sinning or something worse may happen to you*' (John 5:1-14). Jesus had healed him but the man was unaware his sickness was due to sin. Jesus warned that he mustn't turn back to his sin or he may be worse than before.

'*Praise the Lord, who **forgives** all your sins **and heals** all your diseases*' (Psalm 103:3). In the Old Testament, forgiveness was known to release physical healing. The Lord said to His people that if they listened to Him and did what was right in His eyes, obeying His commands, then no sickness or disease would fall on them (Exodus 15:26).

Jesus demonstrated clearly how the forgiveness of sin was required in order to bring physical healing to both the paralysed and crippled men.

7) *Compassion*

Jesus had *compassion on **all** He healed. '*Jesus went through all the towns and villages, teaching in the synagogues, preaching the good news of the Kingdom and **healing every disease and sickness**. When He saw the crowds, **He had compassion on them**'* (Mathew 9:35, 14:14 & 20:34). **Filled with compassion**, Jesus reached out His hand, touched the man with leprosy and said, 'Be clean!' (Mark 1:41). The word leprosy was also used to refer to unclean or diseased skin. To touch a man with leprosy (or unclean, diseased skin) was an act of love and compassion.

Com-passion is reaching out to people 'with love' or 'with a passion' for them to be healed or set free. Jesus wasn't afraid of encountering demonic spirits; they were afraid of Him and what He was going to do with them. Likewise, we are to show compassion to those who want to be healed and set free emotionally, mentally and spiritually. Compassion releases the Spirit of God through which healing takes place.

8) *Binding & Loosening*

Jesus instructed demonic spirits to '*Be quiet!*' and then commanded them to leave the person by saying, '*Come out of him!*' (Mark 1:25). This is binding and casting out. Jesus spoke few words but, because the words were spoken with authority, they were very powerful and effective. We too can command any manifesting spirit or demon to be quiet and stop manifesting, before ordering it to leave the person's body in Jesus' Name. As already mentioned, it's not about how many words we say; it's about the spiritual authority we carry and commanding the evil spirit out of the person.

When Jesus spoke to Peter, He gave him the keys of the Kingdom of Heaven to bind and loosen on earth as it is in Heaven. That is to bind on earth what has already been bound in Heaven and loosen on earth what has already been loosened in Heaven (Mathew 16:19). Jesus later repeated the same message to a wider audience, '*I tell you the truth, whatever you bind on earth will be bound in heaven, and whatever you loose on earth will be loosed in heaven*' (Mathew 18:18). We know that there is no sickness or disease in Heaven, so we can bind sickness on earth and loosen healing as it is in Heaven. It is like when we pray, Your Kingdom come Your will be done *on earth as in heaven*.

On one occasion, Jesus asked a demon-possessed man, '*What is your name?*' The demon replied, '*My name is Legion, for we are many*' (Mark 5:9). It is not clear here if Jesus was speaking to the demon or to the man when he asked, 'What is your name?' for it says in the previous verse that Jesus had already commanded the evil spirit to come out of this man. However, other cases reveal Jesus approaching demons differently. It says demons came out of many people shouting, 'You are the Son of God!' But it then says Jesus rebuked them and wouldn't allow them to speak, because they knew He was the Christ. This shows that He refused to have conversation with them for He ordered them to be quiet first before then commanding them to come out of the person (Luke 4:41, Mark 1:25).

Jesus would address the evil spirit by referring to what function it did. In one person, He commanded a deaf and mute spirit to leave and in another He cast out a spirit of infirmity. '*He rebuked the evil spirit. "**You deaf and mute spirit.** I command you, come out of him and **never enter him again**"*' (Mark 9:25). He spoke differently when, '*A woman was there who had been **crippled by a spirit** for eighteen years. She was bent over and could not straighten up at all. Jesus said, "Woman, you are **set free from your infirmity**"*' (Luke 13:11-13).

I don't believe it is necessary to speak to demons to find out who they are before commanding them out of individuals.

This is only giving them unnecessary attention. We can always rely on the Holy Spirit to give us the knowledge and discernment we need when setting someone free from an evil spirit. When we are aware that there could be an evil spirit behind someone's illness, we can speak to it by binding the spirit behind the symptoms, then commanding it to leave in Jesus' Name.

9) Healing from a Distance

Jesus was impressed by the centurion's faith that knew if Jesus just said the word, his servant would be healed. Here the faith of the centurion released healing even though it was from a distance to where Jesus was standing (Mathew 8:8).

Jesus healed a royal official's son who was sick. The man begged Jesus to come with him for his son was dying but Jesus replied, *'You may go. Your son will live'*. Here Jesus chose not to go, but heal from a distance. The man believed and, when he went, he found out at the same time Jesus spoke these words the fever had left his son (John 4:46-53). Likewise, when the Greek Syrophoenician woman fell at Jesus' feet begging for Him to heal her daughter who was possessed by an evil spirit, Jesus responded, *'For such a reply, you may go; the demon has left your daughter'* (Mark 7:29). Due to this Gentile woman's faith, Jesus delivered her daughter of an evil spirit, from a distance.

10) Rebuking the Sickness

On other occasions, Jesus simply spoke directly at the sickness and rebuked it. Simon Peter's mother-in-law was very sick with a high fever and when Jesus approached her, He rebuked the fever and it instantly left her (Luke 4:39). I believe we too can speak directly at a sickness or disease and rebuke the symptoms or illness in the Name of Jesus. We can take authority over the symptoms or sickness as we command the symptoms to go and then command the body or organs to be healed. This isn't necessarily commanding a demon to go, but rather commanding the body itself to be healed. It is simply taking spiritual authority over sickness, just like Jesus demonstrated. When Jesus healed the man who was deaf and couldn't speak, He commanded the man's ears to, *'Be opened!'* (Mark 7:34).

Some times and for no apparent reason I have suddenly felt a pain in a part of my body especially when walking. However, as soon as I have taken authority over the symptom and rebuked it, within seconds or minutes, it has left me. I believe we have authority over our bodies and can command the symptoms to go instead of accepting them and labelling ourselves with an illness.

Jesus never took sick. I believe it was because He was without sin but also because He walked in complete authority. Every demon and sickness had to surrender to Him. None were allowed to enter Him. Since Jesus carried God's Presence with power and anointing, He was essentially bringing Heaven to earth. Since there is no sickness in Heaven, then this meant sickness had to flee when meeting His Presence.

11) *Raising the Dead*
Jesus demonstrated that He had power and authority to raise the dead. He said, *'I am the Resurrection and the Life. He who believes in Me will live, even though he dies; and whoever lives and believes in Me will never die'*. Jesus then prays aloud to His Father, thanking Him and bearing witness that God has sent Him. He then, with authority, calls Lazarus to come forth from the burial tomb and *'the dead man came out, his hands and feet wrapped with strips of linen, and a cloth around his face'* (John 11:25-43).

On another occasion, Jesus raised a widow's son from the dead. He simply ordered the young man to get up from the coffin: *'Young man, I say to you, get up!'* After Jesus touched the coffin and spoke these words *'the dead man sat up and began to talk'* (Luke 7:14). Another time, Jesus was approached by a synagogue ruler named Jairus, for his daughter had died. Jesus told Jairus, *'Don't be afraid; just believe and she will be healed'*. Jesus then went to his daughter and said, *'"My child, get up!" Her spirit returned and at once she stood up'* (Mathew 9:18-24, Luke 8:49-55).

On all three occasions when Jesus raised these people from the dead, He ordered or commanded them to get up or come forth. When He did, their spirits returned to their bodies and life was breathed back in them again. It is interesting from a medical point of view that apparently the spirit leaves the body

97

when someone dies and, as it states in scripture when the spirit returned to the girl, she came back to life. This is what the Lord spoke to Ezekiel in the Valley of Dry Bones, *'Prophesy to these bones and say to them, "Dry bones, hear the word of the Lord! This is what the Sovereign Lord says to these bones: **I will make breath enter you and you will come to life.**"'* It was only as breath entered these slain bodies, that they came back to life (Ezekiel 37: 4-10). Jesus is our resurrection and our life. He said, *'The Spirit gives life; the flesh counts for nothing. The words I have spoken to you are Spirit and they are life'* (John 6:63).

12) Obedience and Availability

Jesus came to **do the will** of His Father (John 6:38, Mathew 7:21). He only did **what He saw or heard** Him doing (John 5:19, 30) and **spoke only** what the **Father had taught Him** (John 8:28). Yet, He never said no or refused anyone healing though some had to shout louder to be heard in a crowd, like the blind man saying *'Jesus, Son of David, have mercy on me'* or the Gentile woman who persisted in her faith until He healed her daughter (Mathew 20:29-31, 15:21-28).

In the evening, Jesus was still healing the sick. *'When evening came, **many** who were demon-possessed were brought to Him and He **drove out** the **spirits with a word** and healed **all** the sick'* (Mathew 4:23, 8:16). Jesus said that the words He speaks are not His own, rather it is the **Father living in Him that is doing the work** (John 14:10). We are to *speak His word* of healing and deliverance as His Spirit leads, but not forget it is God who *does the work!*

Jesus made Himself available to those who came across His path or to those whom His Father sent Him to minister to. Jesus demonstrated an attitude of humility and a servant heart in all that He did. He told His disciples that He came to serve and not be served when they asked who was the greatest (Luke 22:27). He later demonstrated this through the washing of His disciples' feet (John 13:1-17).

13) Revelation & Discernment

Jesus had revelation and discernment as to what the problem was in the person's life. He could see if the sickness was due to natural causes, if it was due to sin or if there was a demonic spirit causing it. He always took the next steps as His Father instructed, since He didn't heal those with the same sickness the same way. Revelation and discernment came with the anointing and power that was upon Him.

HOW DID THE APOSTLES HEAL THE SICK?
1) Authority & Power

Jesus gave the disciples *power* and *authority* to drive out all demons and to cure diseases (Luke 9:1-2). He affirmed this when they returned to Him with testimonies of the healings and miracles they had witnessed. They said, *'Lord, even the demons submit to us in Your Name'.* Jesus replied, *'I saw Satan fall like lightning from Heaven. I have given you* **authority to trample on snakes and scorpions and to overcome all the power of the enemy; nothing will harm you'** (Luke 10:17-20, Mark 6:7, Mathew 10:8).

The disciples had come under the same authority and power which Jesus was carrying when they worked with Him during His three years of ministry. This was a corporate authority, one which Jesus released to them as they worked alongside Him. Then came the time when they needed to receive it also for themselves in order to continue ministering under this same authority and power. Jesus said, *'Unless I go away, the Counsellor will not come to you; but if I go, I will send Him to you…. He will guide you in all truth'* (John 16:7, 13).

When Jesus returned to His disciples after being resurrected from the dead, He said to them, *'All authority in Heaven and on earth has been given to Me'* (Mathew 28:18). If Jesus has **all** authority, then that means Satan has none. Satan has power, but no authority since he is a fallen angel and no longer in the Kingdom of God or under the authority of God. Authority in a designated area can only be given to us by the one whose authority in that area we are willing to submit to. If we surrender our lives to God and submit our will to Him, He will release His authority and power upon us as He sends us His Holy Spirit to be with us. Jesus gave His disciples *authority* that would overcome *all* the *power* of the enemy.

2) Anointing & Commissioning

Jesus said to His disciples, *'I am going to send you what My Father has promised; but **stay** in the city until you have been **clothed with power from on high'** (Luke 24:49). Luke further records in the book of Acts that Jesus appeared to them over a period of forty days. On one occasion He gave them this command, *'Do not leave Jerusalem, but wait for the gift My Father has promised... in a few days you will be **baptized with the Holy Spirit'** (Acts 1:4-5). He continues and says, *'But you will **receive power when the Holy Spirit comes on you'** (Acts 1:8).

The Greek word used here for power is *'dunamis'* which means dynamite or miraculous power. It was an explosive power that they were going to receive. This baptism of the Holy Spirit was going to empower the disciples for their work ahead, but they had to 'wait' for it. It was only when the *power of the Holy Spirit rested on them at Pentecost* that they were now under the *anointing* of the Holy Spirit and **ready** to be sent out.

*'When the day of Pentecost came, they were all together in one place. **Suddenly** a **sound like the blowing of a violent wind** came from Heaven and filled the whole house where they were sitting. They saw what seemed to be **tongues of fire** that separated and **came to rest on each of them**. All of them were **filled with the Holy Spirit** and began to **speak in other tongues** as the Spirit enabled them'* (Acts 2:1-4).

It was fifty days after the Passover feast, on the day of Pentecost, when God chose to release His anointing on the disciples and send them out in their full time ministry. However, Jesus first appeared to His disciples on the evening of His resurrection day. As He breathed on them, the disciples were then *filled with the Holy Spirit*. Note that this was the first time when they were filled with the Holy Spirit and not at Pentecost. Also, though they were filled with the Holy Spirit, they had not yet received the gift of speaking in tongues.

*'On the evening of that first day of the week, when the disciples were together, with the doors locked for fear of the Jews, Jesus came and stood amongst them and said, "Peace be with you!" After He said this He showed them His hands and side. The disciples were overjoyed when they saw the Lord. Again Jesus said, "Peace be with you! As the Father has sent Me, I am sending you". And with that **He breathed on them and said, "Receive the Holy Spirit"'*** (John 20:19-23).

Jesus breathed on them and filled them with the Holy Spirit *before* they received at a later date their anointing and commissioning. This happened on the evening of Resurrection Sunday.

The disciples were filled *again* with the Holy Spirit at Pentecost but the main thing here was that a 'violent' wind came first followed by what looked like 'tongues of fire' resting on them. Also, it was 'suddenly'. Here they were receiving their 'anointing' as the Spirit came in a 'forceful' way and 'rested' on them. This was the 'clothing with power from on high' that Jesus was referring to in Luke 24:49. It came in God's timing and not theirs.

Jesus then commissioned them saying, *'All authority in Heaven and on earth has been given to Me. Therefore, go and make disciples of all nations, baptizing them in the Name of the Father, Son and Holy Spirit and teaching them to obey everything that I have commanded you'* (Mathew 28:18). In Mark's Gospel, Jesus says, *'Go into all the world and preach the Good News... And these signs will accompany those who believe: In My Name they will drive out demons; they will speak in new tongues; they will pick up snakes with their hands; and when they drink deadly poison, it will not hurt them at all; they will place their hands on sick people and they will get well'* (Mark 16:15-18).

An anointing is for the work that God has called each of us to do. It is usually received at a later time than when we were first filled with the Holy Spirit. This is because we first of all need to develop our character and mature in our relationship with God. It is God who chooses the timing in our life when we are ready to carry His anointing, for there is a responsibility that comes with it! Just like a father wouldn't give a young child the keys to drive a car until they were of age and maturity, so God releases His anointing on us when we are ready to carry the responsibility that comes with it. Hence, we cannot predict when an anointing will take place. It is in God's timing and He anoints everyone differently. Yes, people can lay hands on us and impart the anointing they carry for us to also receive. If this is God's will and His timing then we will receive it. An anointing comes by the grace of God and not by works.

Many well-known anointed men and women of God have been baptised and filled with the Holy Spirit during their initial years of ministry work but then undergone another *baptism in the Spirit* at a later time. This has been when they have pursued God, desperately seeking His Presence with a spiritual hunger for more of Him. It has also been something that has cost them greatly, including fully surrendering every part of their life to God, including their reputation. Then, in God's timing, He has come in a mighty way. Some have experienced volts of electricity going through their bodies[1]. Others have experienced waves of fire pass through their body[2] and some have experienced tropical rains falling down on them while sitting in a room[3].

John the Baptist referred to Jesus baptising us with the Holy Spirit *and* with fire (Mathew 3:11). Here I believe he is referring to two separate baptisms, one of the Holy Spirit and the other of the fire of the Spirit. Jesus said that He had another baptism to undergo, *'I have come to bring fire on the earth, and how I wish it were already kindled! But I have a baptism to undergo, and how distressed I am until it is completed'* (Luke 12:49-50). Jesus was referring to the cross. His next baptism was a complete death to self, including taking on all the sins and curses of man, before entering a complete resurrected life in the Spirit. We need to pursue God for the next level of baptism He wants us to undergo, but it will come with a great cost. We will have to lay down our lives for Him, and even our ministries, before He will release a greater level of resurrected life in His Spirit on us. Without a death there is no resurrection.

3) Power in the Name of Jesus

Jesus said that we will do even greater works than Him and He will do whatever we ask in His Name (John 14:12-14). He spoke this again later, '*I tell you the truth, My Father will give you* **whatever you ask in My Name**' (John 16:23). When Jesus was speaking this to the disciples, He trusted them as His friends to call upon His Name in a worthy manner. It doesn't mean we can have whatever we want with a selfish motive attached. If what we ask is pleasing to our Father, then He will give it to us (1 John 5:14).

God gave Jesus the Name that is above all other names, that at the Name of Jesus every knee will bow in Heaven and on earth and under the earth and every tongue confess that Jesus Christ is Lord (Philippians 2:5-11). Every living thing has to submit to the powerful Name of Jesus.

Peter bumped into a crippled man and said to him, '*Silver or gold I do not have but what I have I give you. In the Name of Jesus of Nazareth, walk!*' (Acts 3:6). The man immediately walked as he was lifted to his feet. This caused a response by the onlookers and Peter then told them that he hadn't healed the man but the man had been healed '*by faith in the Name of Jesus*' (Acts 3:16).

There was a child who was dying of miliary tuberculosis (that is disseminated TB throughout both her lungs) in Uganda. She was on oxygen and anti-TB therapy, but this wasn't enough. She was deteriorating on the medical ward. We had no high tech equipment available to ventilate her lungs. My heart was drawn to this child so I asked her mother if I could pray for her. Then to my surprise, a spirit of boldness came upon me and I commanded the TB to go in the Name of Jesus! I hadn't prayed for a sick person like this before. Nothing was noted immediately. A week later I was back on the same ward, but the child was gone. I assumed she had died and looked in the death book, but her name wasn't there. I asked a colleague what had happened to her and he pointed to her, now off oxygen on the recovery ward. She had such a radiant glow on her face. I knew she had encountered God and He had saved her from death. It was a glorious moment and I was in awe of what God had done. There is power in the Name of Jesus!

4) *Power in the Blood of Jesus*

It is through the blood of Jesus that we are cleansed, purified, healed and redeemed. John said that the blood of Jesus *purifies us from all sin* and Peter states that we have been *redeemed with the precious blood of Jesus* and that *'by His wounds (or stripes) you have been healed'* (1 John 1:5-7, 1 Peter 1:18-19, 2:24). It is a fundamental belief to the Christian faith that we have been made one with Christ through the shedding of His blood and we *have been* healed by what He did on the cross for us.

According to Leviticus, the life of a creature is in the blood and God had made the atonement of sin possible through the sacrifice of an animal on the altar. It is the blood that makes atonement for one's life (Leviticus 17:11). There is life in the blood and it is through the blood of Jesus that our sins have now been atoned for (Hebrews 2:17).

Isaiah 53:4-5 says: *'Surely He took up our **infirmities** and carried our **sorrows,** yet we considered Him stricken by God, smitten by Him and afflicted. But He was pierced for our **transgressions,** He was crushed for our **inequities;** the punishment that brought us peace was upon Him and **by His wounds we are healed'.** The Hebrew word for 'infirmities' (or 'grief') is *'choliy'*. This means sickness, but also can mean anxiety. So 'infirmities' translates as physical and emotional sickness. The Hebrew word for 'sorrow' is *'mak'ob'* and means pain or anguish. Transgressions and inequities both refer to sin but are translated differently in Hebrew. The Hebrew word for 'transgressions' is *'pesha'* which means to revolt or rebel. Whereas the Hebrew word for 'inequity' is *'avon'* which means twisted, distorted, perversity or punishment of iniquity. This scripture is also referred to in Mathew 8:16-17: *'Many who were demon-possessed were brought to Him and He drove out the spirits with a word and healed all the sick. This was to fulfil what was spoken through the prophet Isaiah: "He took up our infirmities and carried our diseases"'.* Essentially what is written in Isaiah and Mathew is that the blood of Jesus not only forgives our sins but also heals us physically and emotionally as well as delivers us of demonic spirits.

One day while I was out walking, the Holy Spirit was speaking to me about the blood of Jesus. So I asked God to show me what it would feel like to have a drop of His blood fall on me. I received it by faith and within minutes my body felt intensely pure and super clean throughout. I felt like a bride, spotless and beautiful in every cell of my body. It was an amazing experience and this was just from one drop of His blood! I understood how His blood really does sanctify our bodies. It was like supernatural bleach killing everything inside and one clean holy vessel was left. There is power when we ask for the cleansing of His blood on our bodies where it has been polluted by sickness and sin.

At the last supper with His disciples, Jesus took bread, broke it and gave it to His disciples saying, *'This is My body* given to you; do this in remembrance of Me'. After the supper He took the cup saying, '*This **cup is the new covenant in My blood** which is poured out for you*' (Luke 22:19-21). In Mathew's version it reads, '***This is My blood** of the covenant, which is poured out for many for the **forgiveness of sins**'* (Mathew 26:28).

Jesus is clear in what He says. He doesn't say, 'this represents' or 'this is symbolic', but He says in all accounts, 'THIS IS'. I don't believe we are to take communion out of a sense of religious duty, but we are to take the body and blood of Christ in a worthy manner. This involves repenting of any sin and then asking Jesus to cleanse our body, soul and spirit with His precious blood. I believe our attitude should be one of coming before the feet of Jesus and surrendering our very selves to Him (1 Corinthians 11:23-32).

Many have experienced healing and deliverance when taking communion. Many times the Lord has told me to take communion with Him, whether on my own or with a team of believers. Each time has been a special moment where His Presence has been felt. We mustn't underestimate the power that there is in taking communion. It is more than eating bread and drinking juice or wine. As we take it by faith in the natural, I believe it becomes His body and blood in the supernatural. The same is true when anointing someone with oil in the natural; the Holy Spirit may descend on them in the supernatural. We must never underestimate the power in His blood. For through His blood we see healing, forgiveness of sins, cleansing of evil spirits and even protection from the evil one (Exodus 12:13).

105

5) Praying in Pairs

Jesus sent the disciples out 'two by two' when ministering to the sick (Luke 10:1, Mark 6:7). The Holy Spirit said to the church at Antioch, '*Set apart for Me Barnabas and Saul for the work to which I have called them*'. And Jesus told His disciples, '*If two of you agree about anything you ask for, it will be done for you by My Father in Heaven. For where two or three come together in My Name, there am I with them*' (Acts 13:2. Mathew 18:19).

I believe there is wisdom when praying in twos or threes. First, two are better than one when listening to God and ministering to someone. One can be interceding while the other is ministering. Two can also bear witness to what has taken place during the ministry time and prevent any unhealthy relationship, false accusation or misinterpretation from occurring. Also, there can be greater protection and support when working alongside others compared to working alone. God enjoys it when we minister together in the power of His Spirit. Where there has been agreement and unity in the Spirit amongst believers, I have seen Him release a much greater measure of His anointing (Psalm 133:1-2). Hence, Jesus encouraged His disciples to pray together in His name, for He would be with them.

6) Raising the Dead

Peter raised a fellow disciple, Tabitha, from the dead when asked to go to her. First he sent all the mourners out of her room and got down on his knees and prayed. He then said, '*Tabitha, get up*'. She opened her eyes and sat up (Acts 9:40).

Paul raised a young man, Eutychus, from the dead. The man had fallen asleep when sitting on a ledge while Paul was speaking to a crowd and fell three floors to the ground. Paul immediately went and threw himself on the young man and he came back to life (Acts 20:7-12).

Jesus instructed His disciples to '*heal the sick, **raise the dead**, cleanse those with leprosy and drive out demons*' (Mathew 10:8). God has given us power and authority to raise the dead, for His Spirit gives life. I have heard many testimonies of others raising the dead or from people who have been raised from the dead, but this is still an area which I am yet to experience firsthand for myself.

7) Humility & Grace

The apostles realised they could do nothing for God without the power of the Holy Spirit. Jesus had already spoken this word to them before His death on the cross. He said, *'I am the vine; you are the branches. If a man remains in Me and I in him, he will bear much fruit; apart from Me you can do nothing'* (John 15:4-5). All they did came from the grace of Jesus; that is, His strength and ability to do what they couldn't normally do by themselves. With great power the apostles testified to the resurrection of the Lord and **much grace** was upon them (Acts 4:33). Stephen too was a man full of God's grace and power who performed signs and miracles among the people (Acts 6:8).

When Simon the sorcerer saw what the apostles were doing, he wanted to buy the Holy Spirit from them and have what they had for his own selfish use. But Peter rebuked him saying that you can't buy the gift of God. He could see into his heart that his motives were impure (Acts 9:18).

When Jesus first sent out the twelve disciples, He told them, *'Freely you have received. Freely give'* (Mathew 10:8). All that we have received from God comes freely, whether it is salvation, the gifts of the Holy Spirit, or an anointing to minister to God's people. We have received all only through the works of His grace. We can take no credit for ourselves but freely give away that which the Holy Spirit has given us and trust God to provide in His own way for our everyday needs. Sadly, many people ask for money for themselves or their ministries when people are healed. Some even require people to pay to receive healing. Jesus gave freely and trusted in His Father to provide for His needs. I believe we are to do likewise. (Let us not confuse this with people who feel led by God to bless others financially for their ministry. God does ask us to give and to bless others, but there is freedom in doing so.)

8) Faith & Boldness

Peter with faith and boldness commanded the crippled man, in the Name of Jesus, to walk! He later declared that it was by faith in the Name of Jesus that the crippled man was healed. *'It is Jesus' Name and the faith that comes through Him that has given this complete healing to him'* (Acts 3:16). Peter and John were then arrested and brought before the rulers and elders where they were told to stop preaching in the Name of Jesus. But they refused to stop and after they were released, the apostles prayed with their fellow believers for an even greater release of boldness to fall on them to speak God's Word. They prayed, *'Now Lord, consider their threats and enable Your servants to speak Your Word with great boldness. Stretch out Your hand to heal and perform miraculous signs and wonders through the Name of Your holy servant Jesus'.* The place where they were meeting was then shaken, they all were filled with the Holy Spirit and spoke the Word of God *boldly* (Acts 4: 29-31).

9) Laying on of Hands

When Paul was shipwrecked on the island of Malta, the chief official invited him to his home. During this time, Paul noticed that the chief official's father was sick in bed. He had fever and dysentery. *'Paul went into see him and after prayer, placed his hands on him and healed him'* (Acts 28:8).

The Lord instructed Ananias in a vision to go to Saul of Tarsus and to place his hands on him to restore his sight. So Ananias obeyed, and after placing his hands on Saul, something like scales fell from Saul's eyes and he could see again (Acts 9:11-18).

Paul encouraged Timothy to fan into the flame the gift of God which he received through the laying on of hands (2 Timothy 1:6, 1 Timothy 4:14). The laying on of hands was used to release healing and to impart the Holy Spirit to others (Acts 8:17). This became a normal part of life for the disciples and apostles.

10) Forgiveness of Sins

James teaches that we are to confess our sins to one another, so that we may be healed. *'And the prayer offered in faith will make the sick person well; the Lord will raise him up. If he has sinned, he will be forgiven. Therefore,* **confess your sins to each other and pray for each other so that you may be healed'** (James 5:15-16).

If there is any sin that has not been confessed or people not forgiven, then this should be done in order to receive healing and stay healed. So often sickness is due to sin not being dealt with in our lives. There may have been things that we have said or done that have given the enemy legal access to inflict sickness or disease upon us. We need to close this open door to the enemy through repentance and receive God's forgiveness and mercy. Likewise, we must be careful not to bring judgement on others who are struggling to be healed. Kindness leads to repentance (Romans 2:4).

11) Peter's Shadow

People brought the sick into the streets as Peter passed by so that his shadow may fall on some and they would get healed (Acts 5:15). This has nothing to do with Peter's actual shadow but it is referring to the overflowing Presence of God that Peter was carrying. It was God's Presence they were coming into contact with and hence being healed. When people are carrying the anointing of God there can be such an overflow of the Spirit of God that the people nearby get healed or even slain in the Spirit without the person even touching them.

12) Paul's Handkerchief & Apron

God did extraordinary miracles through Paul, so that even handkerchiefs and aprons which had touched him were taken to the sick and their illnesses were cured and the evil spirits left them (Acts 19:11). This is useful when someone can't physically reach out to the person who is carrying the healing anointing and the anointed person transfers the anointing power to heal the sick through a piece of cloth for them to touch instead.

13) Anointing with Oil

When Jesus sent out the disciples, they drove out many demons and **anointed many sick people with oil and healed** them (Mark 6:13). James refers to something similar. He says that if anyone is sick he should get the elders of the church to pray over him and *anoint him with oil in the Name of the Lord*. And the prayer offered in *faith* will make the sick person well (James 5:13-16). Here he combines the anointing of oil with a prayer said in faith.

We mustn't have faith in the oil but God. However, the oil in scripture refers to the oil of the Spirit (Psalm 133:2, Isaiah 61:3, Hebrews 1:9). It is like a prophetic act done in obedience to the Holy Spirit's guidance. As I am praying for someone it may come to my mind to then anoint them with oil. I have witnessed many receive the power of the Holy Spirit in greater measure and even receive healing when I have anointed them with oil, but this has been done under the prompting of the Holy Spirit.

A Naturally Supernatural Lifestyle

Jesus demonstrated during His life on earth how we can live a naturally supernatural lifestyle. He passed this lifestyle on to His disciples and also to us. He told us that we will do even greater things than what He had been doing for He was going to the Father (John 14:12).

We too can live a naturally supernatural lifestyle if we choose to live like Jesus and His disciples did, with the power of the Holy Spirit dwelling in us and daily seeking His council in all things. This same healing and deliverance which Jesus and His disciples did, is available for us today!

Chapter 9

HEALING AND DELIVERANCE (II)

DELIVERANCE GUIDELINES

*'God anointed Jesus of Nazareth with the **Holy Spirit and power**
and He went around doing good and **healing all who were
under the power of the devil, because God was with Him'**.*
(Acts 10:38)

**Do you need to be a born-again believer before receiving
deliverance ministry?**
I would like to answer this question referring both to experience
and the Word of God. Jesus didn't actually tell anyone that they
had to become a follower of His before He would heal them. To
some, like the cripple He healed at the pool, He did say later 'sin
no more' and explained that if he did sin, he would be worse off
(John 5:14). To the lady who had been crippled by a spirit for
eighteen years, Jesus simply healed her from the spirit of
infirmity (Luke 13:11).

While it is Biblically acceptable to heal and deliver a
person without them stepping into the Kingdom of God first, it is
also recommended that they accept Jesus as their Lord and
Saviour ideally at the beginning or after they have been delivered.
The reason isn't one of religion or forcing others to be Christians,
but there is wisdom in it and future protection for the person.

Jesus addressed this in Luke 11:24 when He said, *'When an
evil spirit comes out of a man, it goes through arid places seeking rest
and does not find it. Then it says, "**I will return to the house I left**".
When it arrives it finds the house swept clean and put in order. Then it
goes and takes **seven other spirits more wicked than itself**, and they*

go in and live there. And the final condition of the **man is worse than the first'.** Here, Jesus is referring to our own bodies as being spiritual houses and saying when we command an evil spirit to leave a person, we need to invite the Holy Spirit to fill that 'empty' place so no other evil spirits worse than the first can enter back into the person's 'spiritual cleaned out house'.

I have seen people being healed and delivered without accepting Jesus in their lives. This has especially been on the island outreaches to the people of other faiths when God just wanted me to love them and pray for their physical needs, including setting them free. But when I did the inland outreaches, I felt more strongly to draw people into the Kingdom of God first (by repenting and asking Jesus into their lives) before I prayed for them and freed them from demonic spirits. This was true for the lady who started demonically manifesting when she was prayed for and then started to lose consciousness. At this point, I stopped the demon manifesting by binding the spirit and commanding her to come back into conscious level in Jesus' Name. When she regained her consciousness, she then agreed to accept Jesus into her life and was now in a position of spiritual authority to renounce the evil spirit herself. Subsequently, she was set free with no further demonic manifestations! She was then able to receive His love and be filled with the Holy Spirit.

It is much easier to deliver someone from a demonic spirit if they themselves are willing to take responsibility by repenting of it and then commanding it to leave them. I believe it can then be cast out with minor or no manifestations when done this way. If the person doesn't want the demonic spirit to leave them, then I don't think there is much point in praying for them; for it will either manifest and be such a battle to come out or, if it does leave the person, there is a high chance it will re-enter again unless the person repents and changes their lifestyle. This was the case with the old lady on the island with her bent double back. She was initially healed by God's love and mercy, but her problem returned when she wasn't willing to renounce the spirit of bitterness and unforgiveness.

The old lady who started having 'fits' on the island greatly benefitted from the knowledge that she had the spiritual authority since accepting Jesus in her life. She was now in a position to rebuke this spirit causing her 'fits' and in doing so stay free and healthy.

It may be that God leads us to set people free first and then lead them to Jesus. We need to be wise and obedient to whatever the Spirit is telling us to do at that moment in time.

Manifestations

These may be from three sources. They may be from the Holy Spirit, they may be demonic or they can be of the flesh (that is, fake).

When a demonic spirit is aroused, it may start to manifest especially if it is under the threat of being cast out of someone's body. However, it is also true to say that people can be delivered of demons without any manifestations at all. This was witnessed in the mobile clinic.

Manifestations of demonic spirits can be minor or major. Minor ones may include feelings of nausea, vomiting, sneezing, yawning, burping (usually a foul smell may come out), spitting, sighing, fluttering of eyes, tear formation, coughing, hot and cold sensations, dizziness or sudden headache. The demons usually leave through orifices in the body and the individual then starts feeling better or comments on having 'felt something leave their bodies' from the area that was affected.

Major manifestations may include violent actions, writhing about on the floor, 'fits', change of voice (usually deep and evil sounding), screams, hissing noises, foul language, rolled back eyes and loss of consciousness. The person is usually not aware of any major manifestation after it has taken place for it was the demonic spirit that was in control of their bodies. Also demons try to control the person's consciousness by making them unconscious.

It's important to love the person as you take authority over the demon and bind it in Jesus' Name, commanding it to be quiet and stop manifesting. If they are losing consciousness or are unconscious, then bind the spirit and command them to come back to conscious level in Jesus' Name. Command them to open their eyes if shut and get them into a more comfortable upright position if not already in one. Then you can lead them into repentance prayer (and ideally to accept Jesus in their lives if they haven't already done so) before getting them to take responsibility and renounce the spirit for themselves. I believe one of the reasons people lose consciousness when they are demonically manifesting is because the demon doesn't want them to be in control and take responsibility over their situation.

If the person is struggling to be set free, then you can decide to do one of two things. You can bless them, stop going any further and seek help from a pastor or others experienced in this area of ministry; or you can ask the Holy Spirit for further revelation and wisdom into what is happening or hindering the deliverance and where to next direct the prayers.

Sometimes it may be that you are also dealing with emotional hurts and pain and other times there may be a cluster of demons that need to come out one by one. For example, a major spiritual root of fear may also be linked to spirits of rejection, abandonment and loneliness; or a spirit of unforgiveness may be linked to spirits of anger, resentment, bitterness and hatred. Spiritual discernment is needed in dealing with such cases that may not seem so straightforward. It will be different for each person.

Just as Jesus sent His disciples out in twos or threes to minister to the sick, so it is wise to have another relatively experienced Christian alongside you when doing healing that requires deliverance ministry (unless you are very experienced yourself or training others in this ministry). When I have had no alternative, I have prayed for people on my own but I seek a helper if possible. This is especially if I am praying for someone of the opposite sex. The purpose is to minimise any counterattack from the enemy and can be helpful for another person to discern or bear witness to what they see happening in the spiritual and emotional realm of the person receiving ministry.

When a person is experiencing the Holy Spirit they may feel a much lighter feeling in their bodies along with the peace, joy and the love of God. Other manifestations of the Holy Spirit include feeling hot and sweaty (I have seen some perspire greatly with droplets of sweat falling down their body when receiving the fire of the Holy Spirit), fluttering eyes or tears of joy. Some experience a tingling sensation; others feel rods of electricity through their body. Some feel weak at the legs and want to lie down; others break out into holy laughter. Some may start to shake as the Holy Spirit is on them. All this is good when God is at work in them.

There needs to be spiritual discernment for any manifestation witnessed. Is this an evil spirit which needs to be bound and come out? Is it the Holy Spirit ministering healing to the person? Or, is the person simply faking it and wanting attention? If it is the latter, then we just need to quietly whisper in their ear that they can stop what they are doing and get up or take them to a place where less attention is given. Note that a person may be delivered of a demon without any manifestation, just like a person can be filled with the Holy Spirit without any manifestation.

We must also discern if we should get involved with the people who need ministry. Sometimes we are not to get involved and are to leave it to others whom God has appointed. Other times we may need to fast and pray beforehand. Some people may want to be healed from a sickness but are unwilling to acknowledge and renounce the spirit linked to the sickness. In this case, I would bless them and not minister any further without their co-operation in the matter. It is difficult to help anyone who isn't willing to help themselves or take responsibility for their own problems.

Spiritual Authority

Sometimes, when individuals who are being ministered to start to manifest a demon, those around them may start shouting at the demon from a place of fear. I don't believe this is healthy for those praying or the individual receiving prayer. I would suggest taking the individual into a more relaxed and peaceful environment with only a few there to minister from a place of authority and love. Shouting at demons doesn't release spiritual authority especially when it is actually our fear arising within us. However, a quiet voice which carries authority can bind and cast out a manifesting spirit. Jesus didn't shout at demons but He commanded them to be quiet and leave, by speaking with authority.

I was asked to go and help a teenager who was apparently 'fitting' on the floor and unresponsive to others who were shouting at the demon to leave. As I went, I immediately saw that the 'fits' weren't genuine and the person appeared to be in a panic-like mode. But they didn't respond to me in the natural so I knelt by their side and whispered in their ear telling the spirit to stop manifesting and for the person to come back into conscious mode. Within seconds they opened their eyes and sat up again.

We need to carry God's love so we are not put off by any demon we encounter or manifestation we see, for we know He that is in us is greater than him in the world. As we carry His love and Presence within us we will be able to hold any fear of the enemy at bay, for perfect love casts out fear (1 John 4:18).

Satan has power since he is a fallen angel, but he has no authority. Don't forget God created Satan, but Satan chose to rebel for he wanted to be more powerful than God (Isaiah 14:12-15). When Adam and Eve sinned, they gave their authority to Satan. Satan then offered Jesus in the wilderness all the authority he *had been given* by man (Luke 4:6). Jesus redeemed all His authority back through His death on the cross. He descended into hell and took back the keys from Satan's grip before ascending into Heaven.

Jesus disarmed all powers and authorities through His triumphant victory on the cross and Christ is head over every power and authority (Colossians 2:10-15). Jesus stated after His resurrection from the dead, that *all* authority has been given to Him (Mathew 28:18). This same authority has been given to you, me and those who choose to follow Jesus.

Jesus said, '*Do not be afraid, I am the First and the Last. I am the Living One; I was dead and behold I am alive forever and ever! And I hold the keys of death and Hades*' (Revelations 1:18). Jesus shared in our humanity, '*So that by His death, He might destroy him who holds the power of death, that is the devil, and free those who were held in slavery all their lives by their fear of death*' (Hebrews 2:14-15).

Demons will only submit to the Name of Jesus if the person speaking carries the authority of Jesus. This was witnessed when some Jews who didn't personally know Jesus or have a relationship with Him, tried to drive out evil spirits by copying what the disciples did. They subsequently became victimised themselves when the evil spirit saw they had no authority to cast them out.

Acts 19:13 says: *'Some Jews who went around driving out evil spirits tried to invoke the Name of the Lord Jesus over those who were demon-possessed. They would say, "**In the Name of Jesus whom Paul preaches, I command you to come out.**" Seven sons of Sceva, a Jewish chief priest, were doing this. One day the **evil spirit answered them, "Jesus I know and I know about Paul, but who are you?"** Then the man who had the evil spirit jumped on them and overpowered them all. He gave them such a beating that they ran out of the house naked and bleeding'*.

There is power in the Name of Jesus only if you carry His Spirit and have His authority. Authority comes out of relationship with God. You cannot self-promote in the Kingdom of God. He releases more of His authority in us the deeper we grow in our love and relationship with Him. *When do we have authority?* The moment we accept Jesus in our lives as our Lord and Saviour. Just like the little old woman on the island who was a new Christian, she now had authority to rebuke the spirit behind her 'fits'.

A greater level of authority is ultimately released to those who seek God and continue going deeper in their relationship with Him. The higher the call on our lives, the greater the cost and personal sacrifice we will have to make; but there will come even greater authority for those who have laid down their lives unto death for the Lord.

Jesus walked and lived a life which was 100% human and also 100% filled with the Spirit of God. He chose not to sin though, just like us, He was tempted. He suffered no sickness or disease or ever allowed an evil spirit to enter Himself. He said that the prince of this world had no hold over Him (John 14:30).

As Christians, we can still have evil spirits come into us. Jesus was the only one who was without sin because He was the Son of God and conceived from the Holy Spirit (Mathew 1:20). It is a lie to think we are demon free the moment we invite Jesus into our heart. The truth is, deliverance is an ongoing process in all of our lives because we all fall short of sin and have to deal daily with being hurt, not forgiving others, control, pride, doubt and fear in our lives. Jesus had to rebuke Satan from Peter just after Peter had given the revelation that Jesus was the Son of God. He also rebuked His disciples from wanting to bring fire down to destroy the Samaritan village (Luke 9:55, Mark 8:33).

However, as Spirit-filled Christians we will not become possessed by demonic spirits unless we give full access to the demonic spirits to reign in us. Sadly I met an African man who had been a pastor and Spirit-filled believer, until he wanted power over man and started delving into the power of witchcraft. Essentially he was choosing to seek power from Satan's kingdom for his own self gain instead of seeking power from God. That is why he ended up becoming demon-possessed. This was how Satan fell from God's Kingdom. As long as we choose God to be our Lord and Saviour and to reign in our lives then we will not become demon-possessed. Since as believers we can unconsciously invite evil spirits in us whenever we sin, it is important to cleanse ourselves regularly with the blood of Jesus as we repent of any sin (what we have thought, said or done that day or the days before) and thus close any door we may have opened up to the enemy.

Spiritual Authority Over Our Body
We all have authority over our own bodies. There is a saying 'you are what you eat'. Likewise, we are what we think or speak. If we speak curses over ourselves or others, then they will be cursed. And if we speak blessings over ourselves or others, then they will be blessed. We must learn not to speak negative comments to our bodies but instead thank God for creating us in His image. And if there is anything that is malfunctioning, then we can command it to function properly in Jesus' Name.

Many times people have asked me to pray for their symptoms, but instead I have encouraged them to take authority over it themselves. For example, a lady came to me with a bunion on her foot that was so painful and swollen it was preventing her from walking long distance anymore. Her mother had the same problem too. So she first broke off any self curses that she made (like 'I have a bad foot', or 'I won't be able to walk ι...g distance again' or 'I hate my foot'...). Since it was a generational problem she then broke off any generational sins and curses linked to it. Finally I encouraged her to speak directly to her foot and command the bunion to shrink and disappear. I also encouraged her to bless her foot to be healed and thank God for it. After doing this she commented with excitement that she could actually feel the bunion going down in her shoe.

In another case a lady had been struggling to eat food, for anytime she ate she experienced upper abdominal pain. The excess acid she produced caused her intense stomach pain and now she had developed a fear of eating. So first she repented and renounced the fear of eating. Then she took authority over her acid production. She commanded her stomach to produce the right amount needed to digest food and spoke peace to her stomach. She then blessed her stomach and thanked God for creating it. I was with her when she next had a meal. She ate it with experiencing no stomach pain. She couldn't believe it. I encouraged her to walk in this authority instead of fear. She ate with no further symptoms after this.

We mustn't accept labels on our bodies or speak negatively about them but instead take authority over our organs and body parts and command then to function normally as God designed them to be, in the Name of Jesus. Thanking God for our bodies and speaking blessings on them instead of curses is powerful. There have been times when I have felt pain develop in different parts of my body for no apparent reason. I have refused to accept it, rejected it and commanded it to leave; then simply blessed that part of my body and declared it to function normally in Jesus' Name. Each time, the pain (or in one case it was numbness down my arm) disappeared.

Spiritual Malaria (or Counterfeit Malaria)
Once I was asked to see a woman who had malaria-like symptoms. Her blood taken on two separate days had tested negative both times for malaria parasites. In case this was a false negative, she had decided to still go ahead and take some anti-

malarial treatment. However, she didn't respond to taking two different types of anti-malarial drugs, so I offered to pray for her. At that time I wasn't feeling particularly compassionate in my heart but rather tired and wanted to get home for it was the end of a hard day's work. As I prayed for her, she felt worse and actually told me to stop praying. I believed her symptoms had spiritual roots which was why she hadn't responded to the drugs and felt worse with prayer.

The interesting thing was that about an hour later, I started to have her exact symptoms. I developed a headache, nausea, feeling very weak, feverish and dizzy. This had never happened to me before. It then occurred to me that whatever spirit was in her could have been transferred to me. Just to be sure I didn't have genuine malaria, I also got myself tested and sure enough it was negative. I felt a peace in my spirit that this was a true negative rather than a false negative (a false negative is when there are malaria parasites but they are not detected on testing). When I sought God, He told me to come into His Presence and worship Him. I repented of my negative attitude and commanded the spirit behind my symptoms to leave. I was ninety percent better an hour later and was completely well by the next morning. What a lesson for me! I had malaria symptoms which tested negative, identical to the woman's symptoms and occurred as a result of spiritual transference due to an open door in my heart to the enemy.

I called this 'spiritual malaria' for the enemy can counterfeit any sickness or disease. Satan can mimic anything for he is the father of lies (John 8:44). He tries to convince us we have real symptoms needing medical attention when the truth is we need to receive prayer, repent of any sin where needed, break off any curses and be set free from any demonic spirit. I believe that the explanation for many physical illnesses which repeatedly test negative on investigation, causing confusion to the medical staff, is that there is a spirit of infirmity behind the sickness which is counterfeiting the symptoms

It was a huge lesson for me to learn when I realised that Satan can counterfeit all sickness and disease. Hence we need to be thinking, especially when tests come back negative or there is failure of treatment, 'Could this be a counterfeit illness which needs healing through prayer?'

Cleansing Before and After Ministry

In the same way that we clean our hands before medically treating someone or operating on them, it is important to be a clean, holy vessel for God's Spirit to dwell in us before we start ministering to others. It is good to make sure we have dealt with any unresolved sin before we start praying for others, so we have no 'open doors in our spiritual home' for any evil spirits to enter into us. Otherwise, we may find ourselves becoming sick or taking on similar symptoms to that which the person had whom we prayed for. Even if this were to happen, we can still repent of our sin and ask Jesus to cleanse us with His blood as we come before Him.

This can also be true when we let others pray for us. It may be that they are carrying an evil spirit and we open ourselves up to them and allow that spirit to come in us. Hence I would advise you to put the cross between yourself and those who pray for you, especially if they are Christians whom you don't know very well. Then you only receive that which is good and from God and that which isn't goes straight to the cross.

In the same way that it is important we come clean and right before God prior to praying and ministering to others, likewise we need to cleanse ourselves in body, soul and spirit *after* having ministered to others. Think of it as having got your hands dirty by doing a medical procedure or some unclean activity and then wanting to wash your hands straight after the procedure is finished. It is good practice to ask the Holy Spirit to cleanse you and your team of anything unclean you may have picked up in the spirit realm, in the Name of Jesus. I call it 'de-sliming'; that is, getting rid of any slime we may have picked up. This has proven to be effective prayer for protecting the medical team during and after outreaches.

At other times, when I have been less prepared before praying for someone, I have simply said a quiet prayer putting the cross or blood of Jesus between me and the person so anything I come up against that is not of God goes directly to the cross and not to me. On one occasion I quickly prayed silently the blood of Jesus between me and a woman needing deliverance, but my colleague who joined me didn't cover herself in prayer. As a result, I felt fine afterwards, but my colleague felt strange with a feeling of heaviness and oppressiveness. After praying for her and cleansing her with the blood, she felt back to normal again.

Staying Healed

It is one thing to *be* healed and another to *stay* healed. It may be that we have been healed of cancer or set free from a spirit of fear, lust, pornography, sexual sin or other addictions but we then need to change the *habit* that was with it. True repentance is choosing not to commit the sin again and a willingness to change our lifestyle.

We must encourage those we pray for to step into a healthy attitude and lifestyle if they are to remain healed. The enemy will try and get into our minds and hearts through temptation, negative thoughts or hurtful experiences. We are to recognise this when it happens so we can say no and stop giving him a foothold in the door to our soul. Once we have been healed and set free from any demonic spirit, it will come back knocking at our door. If we let it in again, we need to bind it and renounce it again and go in the opposite mindset or spirit.

It may be that we have forgiven someone only for the same person to hurt us again. We have a choice. We can choose not to let resentment, anger and bitterness into our souls but to forgive them again and pray a blessing on their lives (and pray for the issues they are personally struggling with). Or we can choose to let the enemy in and suffer with the negative emotional or physical symptoms as a consequence. We need to protect our hearts and minds from the attacks of the enemy in order to stay healed. We shouldn't beat ourselves for failing to keep the enemy out, but rather take action each time we do let him in by kicking him out again. This may take more than one go at doing until we are in a stronger position to once and for all keep him out. Once we have overcome the enemy and no longer let the evil spirit back in (be it fear, doubt, lust, unforgiveness, etc.) then it will stop bothering us.

Having a negative thought isn't necessary a sin, but what we then do with the thought can make it sin. For example, I may have a negative thought about someone but if I choose not to entertain it or speak it out to others but choose to think something positive instead, I have not allowed it in and instead have exchanged it for a Godly thought. The enemy will throw all sorts of negative thoughts and temptations at us about others and ourselves. We mustn't spiral down with them by entertaining them, but instead stop thinking like that, rebuke the thoughts and think in the opposite spirit and mindset.

Paul tells us to pray in the Spirit on all occasions so to keep our minds alert from the fiery darts of the enemy (Ephesians 6:18, Philippians 4:8). Don't be discouraged when symptoms may return after receiving healing, but recognise it as a need to take spiritual authority over it again. It is wrong to think that because the symptom has returned then you haven't been healed. No, stand in faith that you have been healed and command the symptom again to leave you.

It is advised, if a person has been taking any medication and is physically healed after receiving prayer, to encourage them to get checked out by their doctor first before stopping any medication. The doctor can do tests where needed to confirm their healing. The patient can also testify and bear witness to the doctor of the healing power of God. In the exceptional case where the person has heard from God for themselves and knows without any doubt that they are healed, then they can chose to come off their medication. However, in some cases where there may be withdrawal symptoms or severe consequences to stopping their medication (like those on treatment for mental health or life threatening illnesses), I would advise to get checked out by their doctor first and then to have a trial of weaning slowly from their medication as advised by their doctor. If they are truly healed they will have no further symptoms and remain well, but if their symptoms return then they obviously still require the medication. Hence it is good to do this under supervision.

Chapter 10

SPIRITUAL ROOTS TO
SICKNESS & DISEASE

*'Dear friend, I pray that you may **enjoy good health**
and that all may go well with you, even as
your soul is getting along well'.*
(3 John 2)

Jesus physically healed many when He said, *'Your sins are forgiven'*. He healed ALL who came to Him and ALL who touched Him (Acts 10:38, Mathew 8:16, 14:36). As it says in Psalm 103:3, the Lord *forgives all* your sin *and heals all* your diseases. He came to destroy the works of the devil and that includes healing and restoring us back to full health (John 10:10, 1 John 3:8). He came to restore our souls (Psalm 23:3).

There have been times when no matter how much we have prayed for someone to be healed, they didn't seem to get any better or they have even died. We may only find out the reasons for this when we are in Heaven ourselves.

There can be so many inter-related issues taking place in our lives which are having a negative effect on our health, that we need our Counsellor, the Holy Spirit, to reveal if there are any spiritual roots or underlying causes to our symptoms. We mustn't forget that we are made up of, not just of a physical body, but a soul and spirit too. Our soul consists of our mind (including intellect and imagination), our will and emotion. Our spirit is our inner being. Our body, soul and spirit are all connected to each other and therefore have influence on each other. We mustn't see them as separate. If we have a prime physical cause, such as an

125

injured part of the body, then we know this will also affect our spiritual and emotional wellbeing. The opposite is also true. Therefore, I believe it is important to consider a possible spiritual or emotional cause to our physical symptoms. I have seen people with injuries where there has been a spiritual root of witchcraft behind it. Accidents may even be the result of a spiritual attack.

There can be a misconception when people think they are 'resistant' to treatment or have been 'misdiagnosed' when medication doesn't seem to work. In actual fact it could simply be that the symptoms need to be 'spiritually' or 'emotionally' treated first. It would also be cost effective if we were to address the spiritual and emotional sides to our health prior to giving out any drugs or performing unnecessary operations.

Many times as a children's doctor I would come across cases where the real problem was the child's emotional or spiritual needs not being met. A mother brought me a three year old girl who developed acute urine retention. She had failed to pass urine for over forty eight hours. On examination her bladder was tender and grossly enlarged. On further questioning, I discovered the parents had just moved home forty-eight hours ago and had neglected their child during this time. It then became obvious that the little girl was seeking attention or trying to seek control. So I played along with the little girl and gave her a choice. She could voluntarily pass urine in a bowl or I could catheterise her. When she saw the catheter, she opted for the bowl. Within seconds, she voluntarily emptied her bladder and was discharged. The mother clearly saw where the problem was and what needed to be done.

There was another case where a teenage boy came to hospital with a limp. On examination I wasn't convinced that this was real but a cover up for an underlying problem. On further questioning, he admitted there was an issue. He was homesick and hated living at boarding school. This was his cry to be back at home with his parents. The moment this was brought into the open with his mother present, his symptoms disappeared and he walked normally out of the hospital.

During my time in Africa when I was teaching hospital staff on spiritual roots to sickness and disease, nearly all those present had some chronic physical symptoms which were healed through prayer. There were two senior nurses who both had chronic abdominal symptoms. One had undergone a major surgical operation with no improvement whilst the other had undergone two major operations with no improvement. Their level of pain was unchanged. A pastor in the team prayed for one of the nurses and, as he took authority over the sickness, she started to cry and then let out a loud shrieking noise. She then testified to a spirit leaving her body and the pain going with it. She had no idea it was demonic in origin, but was relieved to be healed and set free.

The other senior nurse had chronic lower abdominal pain in the region of her feminine organs. I felt led to ask her if she had any issues with being a mother, wife or sister. She started to cry and said yes. After listening to her issues, she was willing to forgive those who had hurt or disappointed her and repent where she had behaved negatively herself. Then we broke off any curses spoken over her (as a mother, wife or sister) and commanded the spirit of infirmity to leave. We finished by praying blessings on her feminine organs and blessings on her as a mother, wife and sister. She then said with tears of joy in her eyes that her pain had gone. As a result of this revelation, she was going to resolve the ongoing issues she had with her family.

God can heal us instantly when there is a great outpouring of His Presence or an 'open Heaven' with His angelic host around us. He can also choose to heal us through different approaches at other times. This may be because He wants to bring to our attention the real cause or emotional or spiritual root behind the problem. The advantage is we can then go for the root and remove the sickness once and for all, instead of a quick cut at the top or one of the branches which only temporarily brings relief. We are then the wiser in understanding what the cause was and in preventing it from recurring.

Stress

It is well known that stress and anxiety cause negative effects on our body. Stress may precipitate stomach ulcers from increased acid production, asthmatic problems from constriction of the airways, headaches or angina from hypertension, irritable bowel symptoms from an overactive bowel, skin problems (like eczema) and even mental problems. Basically, it can affect any part of our body. Hence we need to recognise this so we don't dampen down the symptoms with suppressive medication but rather minimise it by changing our mindset or lifestyle so we are no longer letting our bodies suffer from the physical, mental or emotional effects of stress or anxiety. Symptoms due to stress I believe are like a wake-up call. We need to deal with what's causing the stress instead of trying to treat the symptoms.

I don't believe the life God calls us to live is to be one of anxiety or stress. This may happen when we don't put our faith in God or disobey His will and instead want to be in control of everything in our life. This is because we either lack trust in God or want to be in charge and do things our way in our own strength and natural abilities. God will give us His amazing peace and grace when we are in the centre of His will, even when we walk through the valley of the shadow of death or whatever storms we have to face in our life. We were not created to walk it alone but with Him. We can choose to do things our way or seek God's advice and do it His way. His way is always the best and we will have His peace and grace to do it.

Likewise, we can take on burdens which aren't ours to have in the first place. Jesus said we are to give all our burdens to Him and take on His light yoke instead. In exchange He will give us His peace. People throw life's burdens at us, but we can choose to give them back to Jesus in prayer and trust Him with the outcome. In the Message Bible it reads, *'Walk with Me and work with Me - watch how I do it. Learn the unforced rhythms of grace. I won't lay anything heavy or ill-fitting on you'* (Mathew 11:29). God doesn't say that it will be easy if we follow Him and do His will, but He does say that He will give us His peace and grace and He will be with us.

Unforgiveness

People don't often link not being healed with unforgiveness. I have witnessed so many people receive physical healing, usually from pain in their bodies, as a result of forgiving others. They only saw the connection afterwards. One lady testified to pain leaving

128

her hips only after she had forgiven her father for abusing her as a child and she hadn't even asked God to heal her hips.

A lady recently came to me with a painful shoulder. She had seen doctors and physiotherapists with little improvement. She had two levels of pain. One level was ongoing and chronic after she fell on her shoulder when her son jumped on her back many years ago. This had caused reduced movement where she was unable to lift her arm above her head. The other level was more acute after she found out disturbing information about her husband. As she forgave her husband for what he had done, with tears in her eyes, her acute pain left her shoulder. She still struggled lifting her shoulder above her head for it had been stiff since she had the accident with her son. I asked her to now forgive her son, but she adamantly said she had nothing against him and it was an accident. However, though she felt this way towards her son now, she probably felt anger and spoke negative words at the time of the accident. So she agreed to forgive him and repented of any anger or bitterness she had felt or expressed in the past to him. Then she lifted up her arm and had full range of movement for the first time in years. She was so surprised and had no idea that her two levels of pain causing limited movement in her shoulder were both the result of unforgiveness from past hurt.

Jesus tells us to forgive those who have hurt us so our Heavenly Father may also forgive us our sins (Mark 11:25). It is worth repeating that Jesus said we are to *forgive from our heart* (Mathew 18:35). Unforgiveness is actually a sin and can keep us in spiritual, emotional and physical bondage. It is only when we choose to forgive the person who has hurt us *and release them of owing us anything*, that in turn we can be released and set free from the bondage it has put us in. This doesn't mean the offender hasn't done any wrong, but rather that we are choosing not to judge them ourselves but hand the person over to God instead. James says there is only one judge who is able to save and destroy (James 4:12). We are not to judge but hand it over to God who is judge.

It may be that we need to forgive ourselves for something we have said or done in the past. If we are struggling to forgive, then we can ask Jesus to give us His grace or an inner strength and spiritual ability to forgive. Never forget, Jesus had to forgive those who betrayed Him, falsely accused Him, beat Him, slandered and mocked Him and then crucified Him. He said on the cross, *'Father, forgive them for they know not what they are doing'* (Luke 23:34). If Jesus has demonstrated that He can forgive those who betrayed and tortured Him then, by His grace, we can also choose to forgive our enemies from our hearts. As we make that conscious choice in our mind and will, then with the grace of God, He will enable us to forgive from our heart.

As we choose to forgive we also need to release ourselves from any hatred (including self-hate), bitterness, anger, judgement or resentment that is linked to the unforgiveness so we can receive total freedom and healing. This can be done by repenting and handing the negative feelings to God and commanding the spirit attached to them to leave us in Jesus' Name. Note that a negative feeling like bitterness, anger, unforgiveness and so on, can have a demonic spirit behind it. It may start off as a negative emotion but, the more we let it entertain us, we are actually allowing the spirit behind it to come in our lives. Hence we may need to also command the spirit of anger, spirit of bitterness, spirit of hatred, etc. to leave us in Jesus' Name. It is a lie to believe that we have a right to be angry when someone has done us wrong. This is self-righteous anger and not of God. In believing this lie, we open ourselves up to the spirit of hatred and bitterness as well as judgment and unforgiveness.

The spirit of unforgiveness may be the root cause to arthritic pain or chronic body pain. I have seen people healed of pain in their shoulders, back, knees, hips, limbs, abdomen, neck and pelvis (basically anywhere in the body) when they have been willing to forgive others from their heart. Symptoms may return after receiving healing but that doesn't mean the person wasn't healed originally. They need to check if they have allowed any seed or access to the same spiritual root to grow again. This is like the lady I saw who was bent double on the island. I believe she was initially healed under the grace and mercy of God without dealing with the spiritual root, but this returned when she allowed unforgiveness in her heart again. When I invited her to let go of her unforgiveness, she wasn't willing for this spiritual root to be removed. She would rather hold onto bitterness and hatred and suffer pain than forgive and experience freedom, healing and peace.

An African pastor had lent a friend a significant amount of money to help him get out of trouble. He even borrowed some to lend to this friend. His friend decided to do a runner and not pay him back. The pastor became angry and was out to find his friend and demand his money back for he himself was now in debt. When he heard the teaching on forgiveness, it hit him deep within. He knew he had to forgive his friend from his heart and let go of all the money he was owed. After he chose to forgive, he testified to being set free from what felt like a heavy weight or burden around his neck, which had followed him wherever he went. Now he felt free for the first time in ages and was trusting God to help him with his financial loss. I could see the peace and kindness of God in his eyes as a result of him choosing to forgive. Forgiveness brings inner peace and freedom as we release ourselves from the heavy chains which have been keeping us in bondage.

Unbelief

Jesus was unable to heal many in His hometown because of their lack of faith (Mathew 13:58, Mark 6:5-6). James says that the prayer offered in faith will make the sick person well (James 5:15). I believe we have to be very careful not to say to the sick person that they haven't been healed for *their* lack of faith. Otherwise we can be judging them. The truth is the faith of the person praying for the sick can release healing as we see many times in the scriptures. I have seen people healed when I have lacked faith that God could heal them. Healing is an act of God's grace, so we mustn't condemn people saying it's their lack of faith or their unresolved sin. God can still heal those with no faith and who live in sin, though healing is witnessed more when there is repentance of sin and release of faith. People can have faith and not get healed or have no faith and get healed. At times, God's healing is not as straightforward as we would like to think it is. However, I think it is good practice to release faith in a person by asking them if they believe in God and, if so, if they believe He can heal them. Then whilst praying, imagine (or see through the eyes of faith) the person with the sick part of their body healed, thanking God for healing them and then let them test out the affected part of their body. Faith put in action releases healing.

I love the story of Smith Wigglesworth who raised a man named Lazarus, who was deteriorating with tuberculosis on his deathbed. Smith was out praying on the Welsh mountains when he heard God tell him to go and raise Lazarus. Lazarus had no faith that God could heal him; neither did any member in his church. They had prayed for him but nothing happened so they all gave up. Smith Wigglesworth came along and prayed for him but nothing happened. So he sought God in prayer and fasted a day while asking seven other people to join him. While he was fasting, he came up against a demonic spirit that was behind the disease. He said, '*I told the people that I would not eat anything that night. When I got to bed, it seemed as if the devil tried to place on me everything that he had placed on that poor man in the bed. When I awoke I had a cough and all the weakness of a tubercular subject. I rolled out of bed onto the floor and cried out to God to deliver me from the power of the devil. God gave the victory and I got back into bed again as free as ever I was in my life*'. He had to contend first with the spirit behind the disease. After overcoming the battle, he followed the strategy God gave him. That same morning, they met up again and held hands with Lazarus, forming a circle around him. Then they prayed silently by repeatedly saying the name, Jesus! The power of God fell five times. On the sixth time it fell, Lazarus started to cry and he had an encounter with Jesus. He had a choice to repent of his sin and turn back to Jesus or die. He repented and cried out to God that God would get the glory. He shook in his bed as the Spirit of God came upon him. Then he got out of his bed completely healed[1]. Here, we see how Wigglesworth had to come against a spirit of unbelief which was amongst the fellow believers and then come against a spirit of tuberculosis which was behind the disease. With prayer and fasting, there was spiritual breakthrough and healing seen.

False Beliefs
We all have false beliefs about ourselves as a result of our negative experiences in life. Some may believe they are ugly, thick or a failure because of the harsh words spoken to them as a child

(whether at home or at school). Due to negative experien
others, some may believe no one likes them, that they are ..
or that no one wants to listen to them. Some may believe life is
about achievement and success and to strive in their work. There
are many things that we have believed about ourselves that are
simply not true for they are not from God or how He sees us. If we
are not careful, these false beliefs or negative words that we may
speak over ourselves may become a self-fulfilling prophecy. For
example, we may think and say to others, 'I will never be good at
anything. I will always be a failure'. Sure enough, that is what
happens because we have spoken this negative word and opened
the door to bring a curse upon ourselves. The source of these false
beliefs or lies is Satan, who is the father of lies (John 8:44). Satan
delights in telling us we are no good, not wanted, ugly, a failure,
will never make it, no one likes us, or have to strive for perfection,
be the best, etc. He doesn't want us to live in the truth of who God
created us to be in Him or enter God's will for us.

God believes in us, even if no one else does. God has
amazing plans and destinies for us. We simply need to ask the
Holy Spirit to show us the lies we have believed about ourselves.
It is good to write them down and then ask the Holy Spirit, 'What
is the truth concerning these lies? How does God really see me?
What does God say about me?' Then write down the truth. We
now have a choice to discard the lie or false belief and replace it
with God's truth about us. It helps to forgive others for what they
have said or even forgive ourselves for what we have said. Then
repent to God for accepting this lie and exchange it for His truth.
Repeat to yourself the truth over and over again until you accept
the truth and are now living in it. For example, a lie may be, 'I can
do nothing; I'm not capable...' but the truth is, 'I can do all things
through Christ who strengthens me' (Philippians 4:13). God
usually speaks His truth though His Word or simply a word from
His heart to us. Studies have apparently shown that it takes three
weeks for a negative thought or false belief to be unwired from
our brain and to then rewire or re-programme our brain with a
positive thought or true belief. Hence we need to keep declaring
the truth of who we are in Christ and how God sees us for a

period of around three weeks. It then becomes a truth ingrained in us, helping us to get on in life.

There can also be a false belief, where people are under the lie that Jesus doesn't want to heal them and they are to live with their sickness or problem. This simply isn't true. Sickness and disease aren't from God but Satan. When we open our lives to sin, we are also opening ourselves up to sickness and disease that can come through sin (Exodus 15:26, Luke 13:16, Acts 10:38). It is also true that not all sickness and disease are due to sin. Jesus taught this to His disciples when He was questioned about the man born blind. He said the man was born blind not through any sin, but so the works of God could be displayed (John 9:1-3).

We have a choice. We can choose to live in the truth of how God sees us or choose to accept the lies how Satan sees us. One leads to freedom and the other to bondage.

Fears & Trauma

Fears usually have a demonic spirit attached to them; after all, fear is one of Satan's main strongholds. Paul speaks of the spirit of fear: *'For God did not give us a spirit of fear (timidity), but a spirit of power, of love and of self-discipline'* (2 Timothy 1:7). Jesus repeatedly said, 'do not fear' to His disciples. There are many things we may fear like fear of isolation, fear of man, fear of cancer, fear of death, fear of demons, fear of failure, fear of rejection, fear of heights, fear of doctors and the list goes on.

Fears may also be the result of a traumatic event in our lives. That is, when we have experienced a trauma, there can be a spirit of fear linked to that trauma that then enters us. Subsequently, we have a fear when we have a similar experience. Or we can have a fear when we have accepted the spirit of fear from someone else. We may be told to not walk on our own at night for we may get attacked. This puts in us a fear of walking alone at night. Another person may fear spiders and their scream makes you also accept the fear of spiders. Also, when we experience a traumatic event like a car crash or being physically attacked or witnessing a death, there can be a spirit of trauma which also enters us. So when we pray, as well as dealing with any fear, we may also need to bind and cast out a spirit of trauma.

Here is an example of a traumatic experience that caused a fear of crossing bridges. One day I was walking with a colleague and we were about to cross a foot bridge over a small river when she suddenly stopped at the bridge and said she couldn't cross it. She then said that she had a fear of crossing bridges. I could see by the look in her eyes that she really wasn't going to walk across it. So we prayed and asked God to reveal when this fear entered her life. She suddenly remembered a traumatic experience in her childhood linked with crossing a bridge that allowed a spirit of fear to enter at that point. She simply repented of allowing this fear in, then renounced the spirit of fear of crossing bridges in Jesus' Name. She welcomed Jesus and His peace into her memory of that situation in her childhood so her trauma could be healed. We tried again to cross the bridge and she walked over it with no problem. Her fear had instantly left and was no longer an issue.

An African child was terrified when she saw me in a clinic. I could see she had a spirit of fear of doctors. She wouldn't let me get anywhere near her and constantly screamed with fear in her eyes. The mother had brought her because of her unexplained fear. With a smile on my face, I quietly commanded the spirit of fear to leave her and for God to bring His peace to her. Within minutes, she stopped screaming and by the end of the consultation, she was comfortably leaning against my side with no more fear.

Fears can be relatively easy to deal with if we are willing to repent and renounce the spirit behind them in Jesus' Name (or in the case of the African girl, to pray for the spirit of fear to leave her). But we may also need to ask Him to come and heal our memory of the trauma. It can help by welcoming Jesus at the scene or incidence in our memory and exchanging the fear we experienced with His love and peace, as we envisage Him coming to our rescue. We can then let our spirit be open to the words He wants to speak into our hearts that bring healing and life, as we receive His love and truth in that situation. God gave us a spirit of love and of power. The spirit of fear is from Satan. There is no fear in love for perfect love drives out fear (1 John 4:18).

Here is an example of a fear mixed with a false belief. I was getting ready to go and work in Africa, when suddenly a dreadful fear came on me of contracting some deadly disease while out there. I had heard of this happening to others and thought, *'What if this happens to me?'* At the same time, I could clearly hear the words, 'If you go, you will get it too and die!' I knew these words were from Satan, for there was fear attached with them and I felt threatened. A spirit of fear had jumped on me and I couldn't seem to get rid of it. It started to torment me and I knew this was Satan's ploy to stop me from stepping on the mission field. Somehow, renouncing the fear only temporarily helped for it seemed to jump back on me again. Without realising it, I had let it back in by believing in the fear. The problem was I believed the lie that I would get sick and die and had to overcome this with the truth. So I prayed and asked God to show me His truth. He showed me two things. The first was to choose not to fear death but to be willing to lay down my life for Him. The second was that, even if anything did happen to me, God was greater, for He could heal and resurrect me. So I had to confront the fear by faith and trust my life in His hands.

The enemy throws his weapon of fear at the very thing God wants us to step into and do for Him. We must hold on to the truth from God and take steps of faith to overcome each fear.

Addictions

There can be a spirit of addiction behind alcoholism, smoking, drugs, gambling, glue sniffing, sexual addictions, or anything else that you find difficult to give up or live without. These need to be recognised, repented of and the spirit behind them commanded to leave by the person themselves. But with addictions, there also has to be a change of attitude and lifestyle so not to return to the habit.

I met a man who was on drugs, a smoker and an alcoholic. He came to us for prayer to get free from his addictions. He willingly repented of his addictions and then renounced the *spirit of addiction* to each one of them. He then burnt his cigarettes and drugs and emptied his bottles of alcohol. When we met him a week later, he said he hadn't had a drink or smoke and miraculously had no urge to return to them. I believe he was truly healed and set free from the spirit of addiction. Now he had to choose not to touch or be influenced by the stuff again whenever he came into contact with it and even change his circle of friends. He had to change his lifestyle from this habitual sin by saying no and not letting it get a hold on his life again.

For some, there may be a wound or painful memory linked to their addiction. The addiction is simply a cover up or mental blot out from their hurtful past. In this case, the wound needs addressing first and allowing God to come and heal their heart with His love and truth. Again, Jesus can be invited into the situation and asked where He was when this painful event happened. Then envisage Him there in the memory and ask what is He is now saying or doing. This can release healing in a powerful way and transform lives.

Witchcraft or Occult Involvement

The effects of witchcraft or involvement with the occult can bring sickness, disease and even death to people. There is no such thing as 'good' witchcraft such as white witchcraft. Any form of witchcraft is of demonic origin for the source of the power used is not from the Holy Spirit. If it is not from God then the only other source is Satan. Satan loves to deceive us, for he is the father of lies. Many people go along to 'faith healers', 'traditional healers', 'alternative therapists' or 'spirit masters' believing that they can get healed and the source of their power must therefore be good. The truth is that most people who call themselves faith healers, alternative therapists, spirit masters or traditional healers, operate from a source of 'healing power' that is not from God. This means that we are opening ourselves up to the demonic realm and are now at risk of 'accidents' or even deaths occurring in our lives. Satan's mission is to kill, steal and destroy. We must never open ourselves up to the demonic realm by seeking healing from a source that is not from God, even if it looks or seems good initially or even if we hear positive feedback from others.

Likewise, many are involved or have been involved in the occult without realising it. The occult is a more subtle way of opening ourselves up to the demonic realm. It is hidden or undercover, for it comes in a deceptive manner. What appears to be a game or a bit of 'spiritual' fun is really a gateway for demons to come into our lives. Examples of the occult include horoscopes, palm reading, tarot cards, ouiji board, tea-leaf reading, séances, story books on witchcraft, dungeons and dragons, freemasonry, divining rods, psychic healing, mediums, crystal balls and clairvoyance…. to name a few.

Even if what we were involved in was years ago and for a bit of fun, we still need to repent of it and break its powers by renouncing it in Jesus' Name. We open ourselves up to the demonic realm through being involved in any occult activity or witchcraft and we need to close these doors on our lives after commanding the demonic spirits attached to them to leave. *'Let no one be found among you who sacrifices his son or daughter in the fire, who practices divination or sorcery, interprets omens, engages in witchcraft, or casts spells, or who is a medium or spiritist or who consults the dead. Anyone who does these things is detestable to the Lord'* (Deuteronomy 18:10-12).

Jesus forewarned His disciples that there will be many coming claiming to be the Christ and there will be anti-Christs and false prophets who will perform great signs and miracles to deceive God's people (Mathew 24:24). Just because someone gets healed or a miracle is witnessed doesn't mean it was from God. Jesus challenged this when He said, *'Not everyone who says to Me, "Lord, Lord" will enter the Kingdom of Heaven but only he who does the will of My Father who is in Heaven. Many will say to Me on that day, "Lord, Lord, did we not prophesy in Your Name and in Your Name drive out demons and perform many miracles?" Then I will tell them plainly, "I never knew you. Away from me you evildoers!"'* (Mathew 7:21-23). It is not about doing good works but about doing the will of our Father and seeking healing power which is from the Holy Spirit and no other spiritual source!

'Rebellion is like the sin of divination' (1 Samuel 15:23). When we rebel against God by not seeking Him or doing His will, we are opening ourselves up to the sin of divination or witchcraft. If we continue to sin by disobeying God, we are opening ourselves up to possible sickness or disease. Hence Jesus told the people to stop sinning so they could stay healed.

We need to be aware that sickness can be due to the effects of occult involvement or involvement with witchcraft. When I have met people with symptoms that seemed somewhat counterfeit, I have first enquired about there being any emotional root to their problem. (This is not uncommon, especially in the field of paediatrics where the child's symptoms may be a cry for attention or love.) Where appropriate, I have asked if there has ever been any involvement in witchcraft, including dabbling in the occult, going to a witchdoctor or being in contact with others who practice witchcraft. Even if we have had no direct involvement with witchcraft or the occult, we must be aware that we can still become victims to the effects of witchcraft. This may be as a result of others (whom we may or may not know) inflicting sickness upon us. We need to be careful when praying for others who are actively involved in witchcraft or when praying over an area known for its practice of witchcraft. This is because we may be coming up against principalities and be overstepping our God-given level of authority to deal with such matters. Before dealing with such matters, we must make sure we are under the authority of the church leadership in the area known for its witchcraft, and also have our pastor's blessing to take part in such prayer ministry. It is equally if not more important that we have been called by God to deal with such matters. If we have been called, then God will give us His strategy and counsel as to how to respond both in prayer and action. My advice is not to take such matters on without having come under the anointing and protection of God and discussed it with others in spiritual leadership first. Otherwise, we may experience a spiritual attack in the form of some sickness or disease because we are stepping outside the level of authority that God has given us. It is one thing to minister to an individual who is seeking healing and is willing to renounce demonic spirits including witchcraft, and another thing when they are not. If people are not willing to repent and renounce evil practices, then we should pray positive prayers asking Jesus to reveal Himself and His powerful love to them.

Let me give you an example of counterfeit symptoms due to witchcraft. I happened to be prayer walking up a hill with an elderly lady (who is also a prayer warrior), when she started to experience symptoms very suggestive of angina. She had never suffered with angina before. Now to the medic, this would all seem plausible for angina is known to come on with exertion, like when walking up a hill and especially in a woman of her age. But there was more to this. We were prayer walking through an area known for its witchcraft. As she was halfway up the hill, she suddenly felt a tightness in her chest along with a constriction over her throat. She also had slight tingling with some numbness down her left arm. With further prayer we asked the Lord if this was true angina or not. It came immediately to her mind that this was the result of witchcraft. As we took authority over her symptoms in Jesus' Name and came against the spirit of witchcraft, all her symptoms disappeared. She was able to walk the rest of the way up the hill with no more symptoms. Interestingly, there is a known history in this area of two ministers who died of sudden heart attacks. I believe the enemy threw this counterfeit illness to stop her praying over this region. Let me stress again the importance of coming under church leadership (especially those with spiritual authority in the area) and the leading of the Holy Spirit when dealing with such matters.

Satan counterfeits all sicknesses. That is, for every real sickness and disease there can be a counterfeit too. This is when things appear to be real but are actually counterfeit, hence medical tests come back normal. It's not that the person is faking it but rather their symptoms are of a spiritual origin, like the woman with spiritual malaria or the old lady who was having 'fits'. We have the authority in Christ to break all power and effects of witchcraft on human life.

Fetishes, Charms and 'Objects'

Before stepping out on the mission field, I was sceptical about objects having power. I have now come to the realisation that objects can carry evil power. Fetishes, which are what the witchdoctors use and give to tie around the sick part of the body, carry power. I have seen people healed when the fetishes have been removed and demonic power (in the form of intense fire) come from them when they are burnt. Likewise, charms and objects can also carry evil power. We need to be careful of the gifts others may give us. There can be evil spirits attached to objects and they can in turn bring sickness and destruction on our lives. We need to destroy these objects so no one else can fall sick with them and remove them from our homes or lives. Obvious objects include dragons, demonic looking objects, crystals or objects meant to make you feel better. Even some weapons may have evil spirits attached to them, depending on what they were previously used for. We simply need to pray and ask the Holy Spirit if they are safe to keep or not, no matter how much we like them or who gave them to us.

A group of people brought back some jewellery after visiting a tribe in Africa. They wanted to give me some of the necklaces and jewellery they had bought from the people. When I looked at some of the necklaces I could see and feel that there was something demonic about them making them uninviting to wear. I questioned them on this and they said that some of the necklaces were made by Christians but others were from the local people, but they couldn't remember which were from whom. I advised them to burn the necklaces that looked uninviting. They had no idea that demonic spirits could be in objects like jewellery. As we set fire to the jewellery, an unusual huge fire burnt from these small necklaces.

The Bible says that the images of other gods (including objects with demonic spirits), we are to burn. '*The images of their gods you are to burn in the fire. Do not covet the silver or gold on them and do not take it for yourselves, or you will be ensnared by it, for it is detestable to the Lord your God. Do not bring a detestable thing into your house, or you, like it, will be set apart for destruction*' (Deuteronomy 7:25-26). This is powerful as it states to not even bring it into your home otherwise you will be affected by the evil powers it carries. Likewise any books on sorcery or witchcraft should be burnt and destroyed. There are so many children's books which have stories including vampires, witches, sorcerers, dragons and demons that seem harmless, entertaining and fun; but they are actually full of demonic spirits. If Christians can write books for children, so can Satanists or those practicing witchcraft and in a subtle way draw people into the demonic realm. We must not be ignorant of this by falling into the deception that it is harmless fun.

Alternative Medicines and Therapies

I would like to add a note of caution here concerning alternative medicines and therapies used in modern day health care. We must be ever so careful to not open ourselves up to alternative medicines or therapies that are spiritually rooted in eastern religions or other life energy forces. Though they appear good and the people practicing them may even say they are Christian, I believe their source of power is not from God.

As a Christian and a doctor, I believe we are either to seek Christ for our healing or go through the natural resources that God has provided which science has proven to be beneficial to our health. Things which are said to have benefits to our health but there is no scientific proof, I would question; for there is obviously another source of power or spiritual root behind them.

God has trained me to heal through using either natural, scientifically tested drugs or through working alongside the power of His Holy Spirit. He has warned me against all other forms of therapies that use an alternative source of power that is not from Him. If we fear the Lord then we should avoid such therapies and seek Him instead. I have seen people being delivered from the spirits behind acupuncture, homeopathy, reflexology and yoga to name a few.

I saw a lady who had pain in her lower back and also taught yoga classes. Her back pain came after she began the classes. She was a church going Christian, yet seemed unaware of the eastern spirits linked to yoga and that one in particular, the *kundalini* spirit, can reside in the lower spine. After she repented and renounced the demonic spirits linked to yoga, especially the *kundalini* spirit, the pain left her back and she was healed.

There was another Christian lady whom I met while in Africa. It came out in conversation that she was involved in homeopathy, reflexology, and many other 'alternative' medical practices for she had a desire to heal the sick. She was under the deception that these were good and acceptable to God, for she had inherited these practices from her mother. So there had been a familiar spirit behind them which made them seem okay. At first she didn't want to give them up, for she would lose her job as well as all she had invested in them. But I prayed that God would open

142

her eyes to the truth. She went away and prayed too and returned to me with fresh conviction from God. She was now willing to renounce them all and never touch them again. After she openly repented and renounced them all and forgave her Mum for introducing her to them, there was a huge shift in her facial countenance. She at first looked a bit dazed but commented she felt something amazing had happened within her. Her face and eyes just shone with the radiance of Christ. She looked quite different. She made a choice to never touch alternative medicines again but to rely on the power of the Holy Spirit. I advised her to also destroy all her books. For the first time in her life, she saw the truth of what was really behind each alternative medicine she had been using. There was such freedom within after she renounced each practice and each demonic spirit attached to it. However, she was now on a new journey to learn how to heal the sick through the power of the Holy Spirit. Her eyes had been opened and she couldn't believe the deception she had been living in all these years of her life.

'Many of those who believed now came and openly confessed their evil deeds. A number who had practiced sorcery brought their scrolls together and burned them publicly. When they calculated the value of the scrolls, the total came to fifty thousand drachmas. In this way the word of the Lord spread widely and grew in power' (Acts 19:18-19).

Curses & Generational Sins

The Oxford English dictionary states a curse is: *'A solemn appeal to a supernatural power to inflict harm on someone or something'.* This may be to an individual or a group of people such as a family or village, a house, church or even a nation.

A curse can come about through sin. When Cain killed Abel, God said his sinful act had now brought him under a curse (Genesis 4:11). God said that if we obey His commands we will be blessed but if we *disobey His commands then we will be cursed* (Deuteronomy 11:26). He then goes on to list all the sins that will bring curses if people choose to sin and the blessings if people choose to obey God (Deuteronomy 27-28).

Jesus took not only all of our sins but all of our curses on the cross. He became our curse through His perfect sacrifice on the cross for us. It is written that *'anyone who is hung on a tree is under God's curse'* (Deuteronomy 21:23, Galatians 3:13). We do not have to live under the power and effect of a curse because by the blood of Jesus we can be set free from all curses. We can break a curse by declaring the powerful Name of Jesus or the powerful blood of Jesus over it.

Proverbs tells us that death or life are in the power of the tongue and also that reckless words pierce like a sword but the tongue of the wise brings healing (Proverbs 18:21, 12:18). James tells us not to be hypocrites who praise God one moment and out of the same mouth then curse our friends and neighbours (James 3:9-10). We can curse others just by speaking negative words about them! Or we can even curse ourselves by saying bad things about ourselves. There is power in our voice and the words we speak. They will bring life if they are from God or death if they are from Satan. We need to first recognise when we have cursed someone, repent of it and then break the power of the curse in the Name of Jesus. Since Jesus took all of our curses on the cross, we can put them on the cross and ask Him to cleanse us from all curses with His sanctifying blood.

It is good to reverse a curse with a blessing. Pray for God to bless those whom we have cursed. Jesus said that we are not only to forgive our enemies but to *bless* our enemies and *those who curse us* (Mathew 5:44, Luke 6:28). Paul tells us to not repay evil for evil but overcome evil by doing good (Romans 12:12-21). A blessing is a weapon of God to quench the effects of the curse. We bless others by speaking or praying that God will touch them and for His love to come in their lives instead of saying bad things which will invite the enemy to inflict evil or harm on them. Pray instead that God will bring goodness into the lives of those who have said hurtful words to us and that He will help change them and reveal His love.

On one occasion I became ill within twenty-four hours of arriving back in Africa. I felt weak and lethargic, with a low grade fever and persistent nausea. I thought that I must have caught an infection from the flight. No medication I took seemed to help me. I asked a fellow missionary to pray for me. As she broke a curse over me in Jesus' Name, my spirit responded and my body started to feel better instantly. I had been under some curse the moment I stepped on the African soil. Praise God that we can break curses with the power of His Name and through the power of His blood. We simply need to be aware that curses are real and exist in everyday life and can be behind sickness or disease.

Proverbs also says that an undeserved curse doesn't come to rest (Proverb 26:2). In other words, if we remain without sin and keep ourselves clean and pure before the Lord, then any curse or word spoken against us will not be able to harm us. So we must be very careful not to open the door to sin and curses by judging others or speaking negatively about others.

One day I was chatting to a lady in my church and she said she had suddenly gone deaf in both ears and couldn't hear me. I thought that was strange and could tell by the content of her conversation with me that she had probably been speaking curses over herself or others had said negative words to her like 'you deaf bat'. I refused to accept she was deaf and told her I thought it was a curse and to take authority over it. She repented of any vow she had said against herself (like 'I will never hear properly again') or any curse she had spoken (like 'I am deaf as a bat'). We broke the power of the curse and any vow spoken in Jesus' Name and I blessed her ears to be open and hear again. In case there was a spirit of deafness, I also commanded that to leave her. She instantly could hear and her hearing was back to normal.

Generational sins and curses present in the form of a recurring illness or ongoing problem that is seen to be passed down the generations, affecting our families, churches, villages or even nations. If anything is repeating itself down the generations, then it is probably due to a curse from a door open to sin somewhere in the history (be it church history, family history or national history). It needs to be recognised first, then the person needs to repent of this generational sin through doing what is called *'identification repentance'*, that is identifying with the sin then repenting of it. This is followed by forgiving our parents and grandparents (or as far back as they are aware when it started). Or, if it is something affecting a church or nation, then a representative from the church or nation can stand in the gap and repent on behalf of their people. Any curses that may have been passed down the generations as a result of the sin can then be broken in Jesus' Name. Likewise, command any demonic spirit linked to the curse and sin to also leave in Jesus' Name. Then replace it by declaring God's blessings and protection on the people and their children and future generations.

Nehemiah and Daniel stood in the gap for their people when they identified with the sins of their nation and repented before God (Nehemiah 1:4-11, Daniel 9:4-19). This was so the Israelites could receive the full blessings God had for them, including blessings on finances and health instead of inheriting the curses from the effects of their forefather's sin.

Some Christians believe that we are not affected by generational sins or curses and believe that they are dealt with at the cross when you are saved and become a Christian. How I would love this to be true, but God has shown how we can be affected by the sins of our forefathers and need to be set free through repentance and forgiveness. As we repent of the ungodly things that we have inherited and forgive our parents and ancestors, then we can experience an inner healing, freedom and even physical healing. We can start to live under a blessing instead of under a curse.

One African Christian lady testified (after praying through a list of generational sins and curses) that when it came to 'addictions' she had an encounter with God. God showed her a band around her wrist and told her it was the band of addiction to alcohol that had been passed down her family line. She had authority in Christ to break it off in Jesus' Name. God told her to cut it off her wrist with the authority He had given her. So she did and was set free from any desire for alcohol. Another lady had suffered abuse and many other things that had been passed down through her family. After she repented and forgave her parents and grandparents, she felt a healing within and freedom like never before. She said it was powerful and she had no idea she could be freed from it. She said she felt like a new woman. A pastor experienced such peace and joy with a freedom in his spirit that he hadn't experienced before. He had inherited a heaviness in his spirit from the atrocities that had been committed in his family line through tribal war and conflict but, after prayer and repentance, he was set free from them.

So it is true that we are affected by the sins of our parents and grandparents. If we repent of these sins and forgive them, then God will forgive us and set is free. Jesus speaks of us being affected by the sins of our forefathers. He says, *'Woe to you, teachers of the law and Pharisees, you hypocrites! You build tombs for the prophets and decorate the graves of the righteous. And you say, "If we had lived in the days of our forefathers, we would not have taken part with them in shedding the blood of the prophets". So you testify against yourselves that you are the descendants of those who murdered the prophets. Fill up, then, the measure of the sin of your forefathers!'* (Mathew 23:29-32).

Also, the disciples questioned Jesus if the man born blind was blind as a result of his own sins or the sins of his parents. Jesus replied by saying neither. He wasn't disagreeing that it couldn't happen, but that it wasn't the reason for this man's blindness. If a generational sin wasn't possible, Jesus would have commented on this to the disciples; but He didn't. He was agreeing that it could happen but wasn't the case for this man's blindness (John 9:1-3).

There is no harm, only benefit, when we repent of all the possible sins that could have been passed down to us from our forefathers. Some we may be unaware of but, when we pray, the Holy Spirit will bring those to our attention that we need to be set free from. A way of doing this is to pray through a list of all the possible generational sins known in our culture. (I recommend the book on 'Restoring the Foundations' by Chester and Betsy Kylstra. There is a chapter called *'Sins of the Fathers and Resulting Curses'* which teaches in more depth on this subject.)

Vows & Covenants
A vow is an oath or promise. Vows can be godly such as a wedding vow or a vow made to serve God. However there are ungodly vows which are usually made or spoken when a person

is angry, upset or thinking negative thoughts about themselves or others. We may say things like 'I will never...' or 'I will always...' In other cases, people may choose to make pacts with the devil when they make vows to serve under Satan's power or seek demonic power for self-gain to use against others. All ungodly vows must be broken by repenting of the vow made and forgiving the people involved (or you may need to forgive yourself). Ask Jesus to forgive you and heal your body, soul and spirit. Then renounce the vow and break its power with the blood of Jesus or in the Name of Jesus.

Some people may have come under a demonic covenant when their parents gave them over to a witchdoctor or Satanist when they were a child. Though they may now be Christians, I believe they still need to forgive their parents for making this ungodly covenant over them and break this ungodly vow or covenant which was spoken over them. The outcome will not only be powerful and effective but also bring freedom.

An African elderly man asked for prayer for his lower abdominal pain. He had it for some years and believed it was renal. He had been to the hospital and nothing that the doctors gave him worked. The tests showed nothing. I asked him what happened around the time this pain came. He said he fell out with his father. His father wanted to give his cows to another son so the man got jealous and started to curse his father. His father cursed him back in return. Then this man made a vow never to speak to his father again. This man now agreed to forgive his father and repented for his own sin and feelings of anger and unforgiveness. He broke the vow and curses he had said and then asked Jesus to heal him. When we laid hands on him, he started to cry. He was shaking and profusely sweating. At the end, he smiled and wiped his face. The pain had left him and he was now at peace and set free.

Unhealthy Relationships & Soul Ties

Healthy relationships are bound with unconditional love and freewill and lead to personal freedom and wholeness. Unhealthy relationships may be bound with conditional love, fear, control, manipulation or some form of abuse. They may be the result of sexual relationships outside of marriage, abuse within the families or co-dependency on an individual. There are people who try to control others or are under the control of others and are unaware that this is an unhealthy relationship, especially when it is due to a familiar spirit which has been passed down the family line.

Paul said that we are part of the Body of Christ and whatever we join ourselves to, we become one with. *'Do you not know that he who unites himself with a prostitute is one with her body? But he who unites himself with the Lord is one with Him in Spirit'* (1 Corinthians 6:15-17).

There was a lady who had been involved in so many different sexual relationships that, when she got married, she didn't feel connected with her husband. She said she felt tied to her previous relationships and felt messed up. However, after repenting of her sin, she cut herself free from all these unhealthy invisible soul ties by commanding any spirit linked to her former sexual relationships to return back to the person where it came from. She was now able to enjoy sex with her husband and feel spiritually connected to him.

Unhealthy relationships have unhealthy soul ties. A soul tie is a spiritual or emotional bond between two people. An unhealthy soul tie needs to be broken. We can have an unhealthy soul tie with our boss, friends, church leaders, teachers, therapists or partners. To break it we need to recognise and confess each unhealthy relationship we have had; then we are to forgive the person involved and ask God to forgive us. We may need to forgive ourselves for letting it happen. Then renounce and break the soul tie stating the person's name and command it to go back to where it came from in Jesus' Name. Any demonic spirit(s) attached to the soul tie, also command to leave in Jesus' Name. Then we can also claim back all that which was taken from us in the unhealthy relationship. Finally, pray a blessing, asking God to fully heal us in body, soul and spirit. This is very powerful and freeing.

Healing the Broken Heart

Healing a wound involves removing the debris and dirt that lies in our wounds (like curses, demonic spirits, fears, unforgiveness, addictions, witchcraft, vows, etc.). Once the wound has been cleansed through repentance, renouncing and forgiveness, we need to let the wound itself heal. Wounded hearts need the love of God to permeate through them to bring complete healing and restoration.

Many of us walk through life with broken hearts. Some are aware of this for they feel their emotional pain on a regular basis. Others are not even aware that they have a broken heart or wounded spirit for they feel fine at their conscious level. This is because their hurt or wound has been buried deep at the sub-conscious level. At some point in life, we all may experience hurt or emotional pain of one kind or another. It becomes like a raw nerve or open wound. Unless we seek God to heal this wound, then it ends up being covered up over time as we put our mind on other things like work or relationships. Yet, we will feel this pain or anger when something in our life triggers it again. We say it is like having 'touched a raw nerve'. Anything that we overreact to is an indication of a deeper root that has simply been triggered. We don't have to live with this wounded spirit but can let God heal and restore our hearts with His liquid love permeating through every cell in our innermost being. Otherwise, it will recur in similar situations and will affect how we relate to others and God. We need to release our tears of pain so we can receive His healing love.

Many people have not experienced love in their lives but instead have had rejection, abandonment, betrayal or even abuse. Some have experienced inappropriate love through smothering or abuse. Others have only received love through achievement or that which is performance based. These are conditional. Others have had controlling or dominating parents, where fear was more prominent than love. We may experience negative emotions as early as the moment of conception if the mother doesn't want a baby. All our negative feelings have either a true belief or a false belief behind them. True rejection is when someone has rejected you and not wanted you. False rejection is when we have perceived what felt like rejection but there was no original intention behind it. Likewise, true guilt is when we are guilty for what we have done and need to repent. False guilt makes us feel we are to blame for something that is not our fault or responsibility. The enemy will try and throw on us the counterfeit spirits so we believe these lies about ourselves. This is especially true for children who have been abused (physically, sexually, verbally or through neglect). They believe the lie that it is their fault and they are to blame. Where we feel a love deficit in our emotions, we need to take our hearts and pain to God and let the Holy Spirit show us what needs to be removed from our wounded hearts (unforgiveness, anger, hate, self-hate, rejection, abandonment, feelings of being unwanted, guilt, shame, etc.). Then we must let the Lord pour on our hearts His liquid healing love. He is the one who restores our souls, just like King David experienced on many occasions (Psalm 23:3).

In my gap year before medical school, I felt God had rejected and abandoned me when things didn't turn out the way I expected them to. I dealt with this hurt by blocking my feelings to God and deciding to do my own thing in life. When I decided to come back to God a few months later, this wound was still there and blocking my relationship with Him. One day, the Holy Spirit prompted me to deal with it. I started to cry as I was feeling the inner pain come out from the wound within. I cried out to God, *'Why did You leave me and abandon me?'* As I laid down outside on the grass, suddenly this bright blinding light shone upon me. I was too scared to open my eyes in case it blinded me. It felt much brighter than the sun. A tangible warmth then surrounded me and I heard these non-audible words, *'Ange, I didn't leave you - you left Me'*. I felt such deep love as He spoke to me. With such love I was convicted of the truth. I had walked away from God due to a misunderstanding of something that had happened in my life. He had been waiting for me to return to Him and continue along the path of life He had marked for me. My wounded heart was now being healed by His loving Presence that filled every part of my being. We must be open to let God heal our wounded hearts so we can live in the fullness of who He created us to be in Him. I came to a deeper understanding that God never does leave us or forsake us. It is us who leaves Him when things don't turn out as we have planned or wanted and we then misjudge it as God abandoning us.

Focus on being Healed Instead of the Sickness

We are to focus on what it looks like to being healed, instead of looking at our symptoms and having faith in the sickness. The problem is when the enemy throws the medical symptoms back at us and we believe we have the sickness again. We have opened the door to doubt and sickness has made its home in us again. We are not to do this but rebuke the sickness and claim by faith that we have been healed. We then can walk in the healing and stay healed.

I have heard different people testify to having received initial healing of cancers or chronic illnesses, only for them to come back at a later date. They then have chosen to focus not on their sickness but instead have stood on the truth that by His wounds *they have been* healed (1 Peter 2:24). In Isaiah 53:5 it states that by His wounds we *are healed* but this was prophesied in the present tense before Jesus died on the cross. Then after Jesus' death and resurrection, Peter states in the past tense that by His wounds we *have been* healed.

A lady I met testified to standing on this truth. She was healed of a cancer which came back at a later date. She declared and claimed back her rightful healing that she had already received and commanded the cancer to go. As she stepped out in faith without focusing on her cancer but instead on the atonement, the cancer sure enough shrunk back and disappeared. The cancer appeared to have come back as an attack from the enemy wanting her to believe the lie that she wasn't healed.

We are to fix our eyes not on what is seen but on what is unseen and yet to come (2 Corinthians 4:18, Romans 4:17). If you have already been healed but the sickness has somewhat come back, then claim back your healing and stand firm in faith until your healing returns. Sometimes sickness comes back if we have opened ourselves up to the enemy through sin. Repent of the sin and close the door by kicking the spirit behind the sickness out. We are to stand firm in the faith that by His wounds we have been healed and reject or rebuke all recurring symptoms until they are no more.

After doing some strenuous gardening, I must have overused or even torn some muscles for I developed a severe upper back pain the next day. It felt like muscular spasm but to my surprise it didn't get better after a week but actually worsened. I was in pain with limited movement across my right upper back, neck and right arm for over two months and had never experienced anything like this before. One day, I started to develop numbness down my right arm. This meant that one of my nerves was being affected. I was refusing to have this or accept any damage to my upper back so I there and then rebuked the numbness in the Name of Jesus. It went as quick as it came. As I was praying, I felt that if I sought medical help then I would probably get a scan of my back and be advised not to return to the mission field. Well, I was coming to the end of my mission break and knew in my spirit that God had fresh mission work for me to do. So I chose not to listen to common sense or take the advice from others which was to stay at home. I could see that the enemy had thrown this backache at me to stop me from venturing back on the mission field. It was a test for me to put my faith in God that He would heal me, instead of faith in others. So I stepped out in faith and obedience to His call and refused to give any attention to my backache. It sure enough disappeared and I was fully healed while out on the mission field. It wasn't an instant healing but as I claimed each day my healing and focused on God and His Word instead of my backache, it eventually left me. We are to live by faith in His Word and Spirit and not by sight or negative thoughts or feelings (2 Corinthians 5:7).

Lack of Perseverance
Don't forget, healing can be a process and not an immediate thing. This may be because God is taking us on a journey with Him and dealing with the different layers in our life that need healing along the way. I like the picture of it being like an octopus clinging to us, with the different tentacles each needing to be removed. When the last tentacle is removed, healing breaks forth.

It may be we are to wait for His perfect timing. Some have received words from God that they will be healed but not yet. Others have had visions of when God will heal them. During this waiting season we are to focus on His Word and give thanks and praise that He will bring healing (1 Thessalonians 5:16). It says in

Proverbs that those who keep God's Word in their hearts bring life and health to their body (Proverbs 4:20-24).

We must not be discouraged when we don't see people healed immediately after praying for them. In many cases they will receive their healing after they have left us. We are to encourage them in their faith by telling them to keep thanking and praising God and trusting they will get the full healing. This keeps us humble knowing the healing is up to God, and helps those we pray for to step out into their healing. I have received many feedbacks from different people testifying about being healed later on or the next day. I didn't see anything take place when I was with them but healing came about the following hours or subsequent days. Our job is to pray in faith and obedience to the Spirit and trust God with the outcome, whether we witness healing or not.

However, I also believe there are situations where we need to contend for a spiritual breakthrough before we will witness a healing take place. In this case we need to ask God for His strategy. It will vary for each person, just like Jesus didn't heal people with a similar illness the same way. It may require a period of fasting or praying alongside with others. We must be willing to take time to hear God and press in deeper instead of giving up half way. When people aren't healed either by medicines or prayer then we need to ask God what is really going on. Is there an emotional or spiritual root that needs dealing with first? Is there any door opened to the enemy giving him legal access to inflict sickness? Has there been any situations involving ungodly vows or curses, witchcraft or unforgiveness? Have we overstepped our level of God-given authority and ministered in areas we shouldn't have? It requires an open ear to the Holy Spirit in each given situation and to ask the relevant questions. Some of these questions are:

- *What happened in their life around the time the symptoms started? (Could this be an open door to the enemy?)*
- *Was it associated with any trauma or hurtful event?*
- *Is it associated with any fear?*
- *Is there anyone they need to forgive?*

154

- *Has there ever been any involvement in the occult or with witchcraft?*
- *Are they in possession of any fetishes, charms or demonic looking objects?*
- *Has there been any involvement with alternative therapies?*
- *Does the problem run through the generations?*
- *Have they made any ungodly vows or curses (evil words spoken)?*
- *Have they had any unhealthy relationships?*
- *What negative thoughts or lies have they believed about themselves? Is there self-hate?*

The Holy Spirit can reveal situations that we have either forgotten or were unaware of happening in our life. God will guide us and heal us if we are willing to be open and honest and take the necessary steps where repentance and forgiveness is needed. He will do His part, if we are willing to do ours.

Chapter 11

KINGDOM MINDSET

'Do not conform any longer to the pattern of this world
but be transformed by the renewing of your mind'.
(Romans 12:2)

A visiting doctor came on an outreach and was shocked by the level of poverty and poor health care that she witnessed in the rural villages. She felt helpless that she could do nothing with the problems she encountered and wanted the people to have the same access to western medical care like that available back home. I too felt like this when I first stepped out into Africa so I knew where she was coming from. However, God has since taken me to a different level of thinking and seeing things. Instead of seeing everything through my natural lenses, I now see them through supernatural or spiritual lenses. I realise that we are limited in the natural with what we can do, whether in developing countries or in developed countries, but nothing is impossible with God. He can go much further than what we can offer with our western skills and resources. And we can do so much more as we learn to lean on Him for our understanding and work alongside the power of the Holy Spirit.

Spiritual Paediatrics
During one of my visits back to England, I was asked to give a talk to some elderly people in a care home. At first I didn't see the point of it (partly because I am a paediatrician and not a geriatrician) until friends persuaded me that these people may want to pray for me in Africa. So I finally went along. During the worship time God pointed out to me that these elderly people,

who were also in need of some physical healing, were His little children and He had actually called me now to do *spiritual paediatrics*. This means anyone from age zero to over 100! I silently laughed and humbled myself, praying I would see everyone as His little child. This reminded me of a comment my father made to me on one occasion. He said, 'No matter how old you are, you will always be my little girl'.

I am learning how to become more 'childlike' in my attitude by becoming more dependent on my Heavenly Father and trusting Him with every part of my life. Jesus said that in order to enter the Kingdom of Heaven we need to be like a child, not 'childish' but 'child-like' in our way of thinking and living. This includes surrendering the areas of our life where we still want to be in control over to our Heavenly Father and being willing to be led by His Spirit as we journey with Him on the path He has mapped out for each one of us.

We are all on a journey and if we want to go all the way, receiving all the goodness that God has planned for us, then it is a one-way road with no looking back and daily laying down our lives as a love offering to Him. I believe God has so much in store for us, beyond our wildest dreams, and wants to give us so much more than we can imagine... if only we will make ourselves available to be of service to Him.

Spiritual Blind Spots

We all have a natural blind spot in our right and left visual fields. This is the area where our optic nerve connects to our retina. Here there are no rods or cones (photoreceptors) so we actually do not see anything in this small spot on our visual fields. Likewise we can all have spiritual blind spots. We need friends and colleagues to help us see some of our flaws or spiritual blind spots. These are areas of weakness in our character or attitude which we can't see, that need to be dealt with.

One of my blind spots was the issue of control. I had been unaware of this but later saw how it was linked to fear. I became aware of it when I kept reacting to a member in the team who also had issues with control. At first I thought it was their problem but equally there was a plank in my own eye and I had to deal with this same issue first. I soon realised that the things we react to which we see in others usually reveal areas we need to deal with in ourselves. So it became an area I dealt with through seeking God and asking others for prayer. It was a process I went through as I undid the ties from my past that were roots to my fear and control.

Then a friend informed me of having a spirit of 'false responsibility' which the Holy Spirit revealed through prayer. It came as a complete surprise when I realised that I was not responsible for my colleague's mistakes. Sometimes we take on responsibility for things that are not ours and need to recognise this then renounce any spirit of false responsibility that may be behind it. In the medical profession the senior doctor would be responsible for overseeing the junior doctor's work and preventing them from making any unnecessary mistakes. I was now in a different setting out on the mission field. Though I was the most skilled and experienced in the team, I had to let my colleagues make mistakes and come to me if they wanted help or advice. This was scary at first, but freeing ultimately.

God may not select those who are most skilled to do His work but those who have humble contrite hearts and are willing to be flexible and surrender to Him and others in leadership. Just as He said to Samuel when choosing David to be the next king, *'The Lord doesn't look at the things man looks at. Man looks at the outward appearance, but the Lord looks at the heart'* (1 Samuel 16:7).

We need to be aware of having spiritual blind spots, especially when others point out our flaws, so we can deal with them and be all that God has intended us to be in Him.

Criticism or Honour

This has been such a huge learning curve for me over the last few years with specific areas that God has highlighted in my life. One occasion was when a friend approached me with concerns regarding another colleague. As she shared her concerns, I found myself agreeing with her where I recognised there was truth in what she said. We prayed for the person with whom she had concerns. However, soon after our conversation finished, I felt a heavy, oppressive spirit come on me. I asked God what was going

159

on and He told me I had opened a door to the enemy by agreeing with the negative words that were spoken. Though these words had truth, they were not from Him. After I repented and closed this door to the enemy, the heaviness lifted. What a lesson! Through this I saw that we must be careful not to come in agreement with negative gossip even if what we hear is a truthful comment, for the source may not be from God.

Why do we criticise? It may be that people don't meet up to our standards or expectations or there is hidden jealousy. I wonder, *would God be bothered by what bothers us?* If so, then we need His wisdom and counsel on the matter. If not, then we too mustn't let it be a concern. I had to learn this myself once when I became bothered by what I was observing in a colleague's behaviour. It weighed heavily upon me. Yet, when I prayed about it, God told me to give it to Him and He would take care of it for the person was not to be my concern. When I saw the person six months later, they openly shared how God had been challenging them on this particular issue and had now dealt with it. I was so relieved to hear this. I have learnt that it is wise to first bring things before God that concern us about others before we take any action ourselves.

Naturally, we honour those in authority and power or those whom we admire, but Kingdom honour is about seeing everyone how God sees them, regardless of what we may be observing in that individual. It's not about honouring ourselves but about us honouring others. As we choose to honour others, we choose to love and see them as our Father does. We also want them to receive all that our Father has for them. We are called to live a Kingdom lifestyle of honouring others, seeing them as God does and helping them live out their destinies and callings. Paul says, 'Honour one another above yourselves' (Romans 12:10). One area of honour which Jesus gave special attention to was that of honouring our parents (Mathew 15:4). Regardless of how our parents have treated us or brought us up, we are commanded to still honour them. This is to show them respect for simply being our parents instead of judging them with a critical heart.

I know of a pastor with a prophetic anointing who prophesies over all newcomers in his church. This is not only to bless the newcomer but to prevent others in the congregation from seeing or judging them from a negative perspective. In doing this, others can then see the person as God intends them to be and help that person enter their destiny and calling. This church tries to see everyone as God sees them and can then show love and honour instead of criticism and judgement. We must be so careful not to judge or side with others when speaking negatively about someone for, if we do, we will be putting black marks on them and next see them through the eyes of judgement instead of love.

Jesus taught, *'Do not judge and you will not be judged. Do not condemn and you will not be condemned. Forgive and you will be forgiven. Give and it will be given to you'* (Luke 6:31-37). We are to do unto others as we would have them do to us.

Logic versus Kingdom Revelation

When I was working as a doctor in England, my decisions were based on logic, knowledge, common sense and experience. However, when I decided to step into mission work, my way of thinking was challenged as God took me down the path of listening more to His Spirit when making decisions. Working alongside fellow Christians gave me more freedom to step into this. Many times when I have been asked to medically assess someone, I have started with my natural mindset only to then be led by the Holy Spirit to approach it differently as He puts other thoughts in my mind.

For example, an African lady who was HIV infected approached me asking for antibiotics for her chest infection. Though my natural mindset saw her possibly needing antibiotic treatment, I felt led to pray for her first and come against the symptoms in Jesus' Name. She was at first resistant to this and just wanted the medicines but ultimately agreed to receive prayer. After I prayed for her, she had a blank expression on her face for a few seconds which was similar to when I have witnessed others being set free of demonic spirits. Then she said her pain and symptoms were gone. She smiled and gave thanks to God for what had happened and off she went.

I have learnt not to solely rely on my natural knowledge and clinical experience, but to be open to what God wants to show me concerning each individual. Jesus always looked to what His Father was doing and thinking and was not overcome or distracted by the things He encountered in His life. We have to be careful not to always think from a logical, rational, common sense mindset. Yes, this is our natural mindset, but it can so often be opposite to what God wants to do in our lives and the lives of others. God's will or what the Holy Spirit is telling us may seem contrary to common sense but we must trust Him anyway. God thinks outside of our human box of logic and reasoning and knows all things, being omniscient, where as we only know in part. The more we learn to listen to His voice and stay daily in tune with His Spirit, the more we take on His mind and hear what His Spirit is revealing to us.

Paul said in Romans that we are not to conform to the pattern of this world but be transformed by the *renewing of our mind* (Romans 12:2). That was written in the ongoing present tense. In order for me to experience Kingdom medicine, God had to first take me on the journey of letting go of my paediatrics and spending more time with Him. He revealed His healing power as I stepped out in faith to His calling to do 'bush' medicine. This seemed a crazy thing to do after all the years of training and experience as a hospital doctor. Yet, my reward was witnessing His love and healing power as well as insight into spiritual roots to sickness and disease. What an honour and privilege to have God as your teacher and trainer. The beauty is that we become more like Him as we live our lives for Him and let Him kill everything in us that is not of Him.

As Paul said, '*Let him who boasts, boast in the Lord, for it is not the one who commends himself who is approved, but the **one whom the Lord commends**'* (2 Corinthians 10:17).

There is a sense of freedom as we take on the new mind of Christ, by daily being under the influence of His Spirit in us. As we daily surrender our mind, will and emotions to His Spirit and our heart's desire is to do His will, then we can enter into a naturally supernatural lifestyle.

Chapter 12

KINGDOM LIFESTYLE

'They overcame him by the blood of the Lamb and
by the word of their testimony; they did not love their lives
so much as to shrink from death'.
(Revelation 12:11)

Intimacy & Habitation

While I was sitting at my desk studying for my medical exams, I felt a tap on my shoulder. I looked around and no one was there. I felt it again then realised it was God getting my attention. I sensed He wanted me to stop my studying and spend some time with Him. I looked at my watch and decided I could spare an hour. As soon as I stepped outdoors, His love and Presence surrounded me. Then to my surprise He said, *'Ange, will you be intimate with Me?'* I paused and realised this meant putting God as my number one.

During my time out, before I ventured on the mission field, I had another surprise question from God. I was out having fun on my bike when suddenly He asked me if I would live a 24:7 life with Him. I thought I was already giving a lot of time to God by being with Him each morning for three hours or so, but He wanted me to be with Him the rest of the day and night as well. I was stunned by this but my reply was, yes, if this is what God wanted of me. This was the beginning of a call to a life of abiding in Him.

God is more interested in our relationship with Him than what we do for Him. He made this very clear to me when He stopped me doing any more medical outreach work while in

Africa so that I would spend more time to 'just be' with Him. I couldn't believe it when I had two consecutive cancellations for medical outreaches. This had never happened before. My initial thought was that it was spiritual opposition but to my surprise, when I sought God and asked Him what it was about, He said it was His doing! I questioned why, for surely He wanted me to do His Kingdom work. Yes He did, but it was more important right then for me to go deeper in my relationship with Him. I still didn't understand why He wanted this at such a peak and busy season in our outreach work. Then I realised He really was more concerned about my *relationship* with Him than what I *achieved* for His Kingdom.

I was willing to put the medical work on hold but there was one problem. I had just promised my leader that I was available for whatever outreaches she wanted me to go on. *How could I now say no without feeling I was letting her down?* I asked God to help me deal with this and speak to her somehow so she knew it was His will and not my own excuse. God did exactly that. At our next staff meeting, the Holy Spirit spoke to her about some of the staff needing to take time out to go deeper with Him and she happily released me. There was no explanation needed.

During this time out I realised God was taking me deeper in Him because He had something new for me to step into. He gave me a hunger to live more in His Presence. The more I enjoyed hanging out with Him, I realised I didn't miss my work. This period of 'resting' in Him was something I was to start doing each day and become my lifestyle.

We have so often thought that we can only rest when not working but that is the natural way to rest. Supernatural rest comes from learning to live in His Presence and to carry His Spirit wherever we go. Just like Moses said, unless His Presence went before him, he refused to go it alone (Exodus 33). It is during these times of 'resting' or 'abiding' in Him that we are able to receive more of His love for us and give to others what we receive from Him. We can receive more revelation and insight to solve the issues or deal with the daily problems. We will be able to 'act' in the Spirit to challenges we face instead of 'react' in our flesh. When we are in this place of rest, His peace is with us. When we step out of it, His peace likewise leaves. We can still go back into this place of inner peace as we repent and choose His Spirit over our flesh.

God is never in a hurry. We need to learn to live in God's timing which is about learning to live a life in the rhythm of His Spirit. I remember once arriving at a retreat in 'fast mode' but God slowed me down. He told me to *walk with Him* instead of charging ahead in front of Him. I smiled as He was teaching me to walk at His pace, stop when He stops, sit down when He did and continue as His Spirit led me on my walk with Him.

Habitation with the Holy Spirit is more than being filled with the Spirit. It is when we have created a place in our hearts for His Spirit to come and *dwell* in us. That is what it means to be a carrier of His Presence. We actually make a home for His Spirit to live in us.

The Psalmist writes that if you make the Most High your dwelling place, then no harm will fall on you because He will command His angels assigned to you to guard and protect you (Psalm 91:9-11). We have greater protection when we learn to abide in Him, for we are hiding under the shadow of His wings.

It is so easy to quench the Holy Spirit or make Him leave us by negative thoughts and words, through disappointment and judgment or criticism, or through striving and doing things in our own strength. This is our challenge, to let go of everything that hinders His Spirit dwelling in us and becoming like Him daily as we choose to do His will and let Him abide in us. Our death to self bears the fruit of a resurrected life in Him. I believe the more we die to our old self and carnal nature, the more we will experience His resurrected power and life in us. Being 'born again' is simply the beginning of this journey of a sanctified lifestyle.

John G Lake realised after ten years of being in the healing ministry that there was something more than just healing the sick. So he pursued after God's heart for a deeper intimacy with Him and a life in His Presence. As he hungered for more of God, he decided to go on a partial fast until he got what he was after. It was after nine months that he then received a fresh 'baptism in the Spirit'[1]. Yes, he was already filled with the Spirit, but what followed after a desperate period of hungering for more of God was a specific time when God chose to come in more power in his life. This was God's timing where he received a much greater anointing to do even greater things than before, for God wanted to see if his heart was totally for Him and not the healing ministry. Here is a quote from one of his sermons on the baptism of the Holy Spirit that stirred my spirit to want more of God's Presence: *'Then the ministry of healing was opened up to me and I ministered for ten years in the power of God. Hundreds and hundreds were healed by the power of God and I could feel the conscious flow of the Holy Spirit through my soul and hands. But at the end of that ten years I believe I was the hungriest man for God that ever lived... it was the yearning passion of my soul asking for God in a greater measure than I then knew... My soul was demanding a greater entrance into God, His love, Presence and power. I went into fasting and prayer and waiting on God for nine months. And one day the Glory of God in a new manifestation and a new incoming came to my life*[2].

John G Lake says it all happened one day when he was with a friend, Tom Hezmalhalch, praying for a sick woman. As he was sitting in a chair across the room from the sick woman, he felt a warm tropical rain shower bathing his soul. This was followed by a power he had never experienced before. Suddenly surges of electrical current went through his body causing his body to convulse and be nearly out of control. God told him that he was now *'baptised with the Holy Spirit'*[3]. Following this encounter with God and a fresh baptism in the Holy Spirit, God sent John G Lake to bring revival in South Africa.

I believe God is calling each one of us into a much deeper relationship with Him, one of us abiding in Him and His Spirit dwelling in us. It is like being deep out in the ocean of His love. Then at His appointed time, He will release a wave of His Spirit for us to ride along with Him to minister and reach out to His people. His waves are coming, but we need to come deep into His Presence first before we can ride them with Him.

Calling in Life
A calling is when God calls us to *co-labour* with Him. I believe God calls us to do that which we are unable to do in our own strength

or by our own natural abilities. We simply can't do it without Him. I also believe that He calls us to places or jobs that we wouldn't normally choose or have even said 'no' to or 'not me'. This may be because He is seeing if we will really do it for Him without having any selfish ambition or other hidden agenda. It requires both faith and obedience to respond to a calling.

The enemy tries to block or quench our callings with fears of what may happen if we step into them. I experienced this before stepping out on to the mission field. I had to overcome a lie and fear from the enemy that if I stepped into Africa my health and life would be in danger. This required faith in God and trust that He would protect me during my time out there. We have to face and overcome our fears so we can enter our destiny and calling. Usually the thing we fear most is the thing God is calling us to. The enemy is simply throwing his stronghold of fear at us to stop us entering our destiny and calling.

Unless the Lord builds the house, the labourers labour in vain (Psalm 127:1). I believe that our work is to do His will and that is to build the Body of Christ and further advance His Kingdom. We may do *good works* for our churches or in our workplace but is the source of what we do from the Tree of Life or from the Tree of the Knowledge of Good and Evil? There were two trees in the Garden of Eden and we always have a choice which one to eat from. If we eat from the Tree of the Knowledge of Good and Evil, our eyes and mind will be worldly focused and operate out of our flesh, compared to the Tree of Life which is Kingdom and Holy Spirit focused. Only the Tree of Life is mentioned in the book of Revelation for the fruit grown on it is eternal (Revelations 22:2). I believe we need to ask ourselves the question, 'Whose kingdom are we investing our lives in?'

Do We Put Our Work First or God?

One thing I have been challenged with is that of loving my work or ministry more than God Himself. One day, while attending a meeting at my local church, I saw how we can have distorted views of how our Heavenly Father sees us, depending on how our parents influenced us. I was challenged to ask God to show me how *I think He sees me*. It came as a surprise when God revealed to me the word 'achiever'. So I then asked Him to show me how *He really sees me.* I saw myself as a little girl and the words 'have fun with Me' came to mind. As I reflected on this, I saw how my earthly father was an achiever and I had inherited this too without realising it. I had thought that being an achiever for God was good, but the Holy Spirit convicted me that I had learnt wrong and I didn't need to be an achiever for God. What God was more interested in was that I could see myself as His daughter and have fun with Him. This was a turning point in my life when I realised that my work and ministry was to be an overflow of my intimate relationship with God.

Identity
Naturally, our identity is in the work we do or the family we have been born into. We might say, 'I am a pastor, doctor, accountant, teacher, mother, duchess or duke...' We identify who we are through our position at work or in our family. I had been living under the identity of a doctor. Though I had laid down my paediatrics before going out to Africa, I still operated under the identity of a doctor, for many addressed me by saying Dr Ange. It had become normal for me, until God pointed out that I was living under this identity and had to lay it down once and for all (this was during a time on the mission field when He had asked me to put my work on hold, to stop doing the medical outreaches and clinic and to seek Him more). So I took off my medical hat and gave it to Him and died to it once more for I didn't want to grieve God. He told me that He doesn't see me as a doctor like others may, but that He sees me as His little girl. After all, there are no doctors, pastors, teachers, etc. in Heaven, but there are His royal children.

Many saw Jesus as a prophet, priest, king, teacher or even just a carpenter but God saw Him as His Son and Jesus saw Himself as God's Son. We grow into our royal identity as we develop more as His children. Just like at birth when we have our identity stamped on our birth certificates, it takes years of growth and development to learn and take on what it really means to be a child of our natural parents. In the same way, we learn through our spiritual growth what it is to be sons and daughters of the

King. Since we have all come from imperfect families, we need to re-learn and become familiar with what it looks like to be adopted into God's royal family and start living from our Heavenly inheritance.

If we want to serve God, it is vital that we know our spiritual identity. Only if we truly know who we are, then we will be able to stand firm against all attacks of the enemy. One of the first areas the enemy attacks anyone in ministry is with their identity. This is what happened to Jesus in the wilderness before He stepped into His full time ministry. We must be firmly rooted in Christ and have all our needs met in Him. Otherwise we will succumb to the temptations of power, wealth, fame, security, sexual sin and pride as well as many other sins. Jesus was able to stand against all the devil's schemes for He knew who He was and didn't need to show off or prove Himself to man. To know who we really are actually requires humility. It is the Spirit of God who testifies to our spirit that we are His children (Romans 8:16). As we are firmly rooted in God in our innermost spiritual being, then we will be able to stand against the different trials and tests we will come across in life.

Sanctified and Holy Life

We are all called to live a sanctified and holy life. To live this lifestyle we need to know what the truth is so we do not fall under the spirit of deception. The devil is the father of lies (John 8:44). We become 'unclean' when we believe in his lies and live under the spirit of deception.

One thing Jesus prayed for His disciples before He was arrested was that they too would be sanctified by the truth (John 17:17-19). We shouldn't be dabbling into or seeking 'alternative therapies' for healing but seek the one and true healer Himself, Jesus, His Word and the healing power of the Holy Spirit.

To be sanctified is to be set apart from the things and influences of this world, the flesh and the devil. As children of God we are to be holy, for our Heavenly Father is holy. It says in the book of Hebrews that we are to make every effort to live in holiness, for without holiness we won't see God (Hebrews 12:14).

169

Peter writes, *'Just as He who called you is holy, so be holy in all you do; for it is written: "Be holy because I am holy"'* (1 Peter 1:15).

God showed me that just as I wash my body morning and night, so I am to cleanse my spirit as I get up and before I go to bed. At the beginning of the day I am preparing myself for the work ahead, people I will meet, etc. At the end of the day, I am cleansing myself of anything I may have picked up that is not of God or where I have sinned. We can do this as an act of faith, believing that when we truly repent of any sin, He will forgive us. We can also submit our flesh (body and soul) to be under the power of His Spirit in us.

I believe a sanctified lifestyle includes being transparent. That means we don't hide any sin from God or man, otherwise it will surface or be exposed when we least want it to and the enemy will use it as a trump card. So we are not to let the enemy have a foothold, but let God be Lord of everything in our lives (Ephesians 4:27). John says that if we claim to have no sin we deceive ourselves. But if we confess our sins, God will forgive us and *purify us from all unrighteousness* (1 John 1:8-9).

Like Paul prayed, may God Himself, the God of peace, sanctify you through and through. May your whole spirit, soul and body be kept blameless at the coming of our Lord Jesus Christ (1 Thessalonians 5:23).

Fear God, Not Man

Many of us fear man more than God. We are more concerned about pleasing man or what others may think of us instead of being more concerned by what God thinks. Paul says, *'Am I trying to win the approval of men or God? Or am I trying to please men? If I were still trying to please men, I wouldn't be a servant of Christ'* (Galatians 1:10).

We may think it is a normal thing to want the approval of man but it is a stumbling block to our calling and destiny. God is the one who calls us and approves of us, not man. Do not confuse this with being accountable to others. I believe we are all to be accountable to fellow believers who hear God, so they can help us not fall into deception or disobedience, but instead confirm our direction and purpose in life.

We are called to follow God and not man. Love and serve man, yes; but follow God. There will be people who hate what we say or do. If we focus on pleasing them and keeping everyone as our friends, then there will be compromise to doing God's will. Sometimes what God will ask us to do will be offensive to man. I would rather that than do anything which is offensive to God and pleasing to man. Jesus didn't focus on what man thought of Him or let it distract Him from God's will (John 2:24-25). Neither should we.

When I became a Christian, I was given a scripture which has challenged me to learn what it is to fear God: '*He will be the sure foundation for your times, a rich store of salvation and wisdom and knowledge; the fear of the Lord is the key to this treasure*' (Isaiah 33:6). To fear God means to be in awe of Him and acknowledge His almighty power, greatness, splendour, majesty, holiness and sovereignty. It is being aware that He is our judge and we are accountable to Him of everything we have done on earth, good and bad. If we have confessed our sin and changed our lifestyle then He will have blotted that sin out and remember it no more. It is the sins we haven't repented of or continue to still do that we will be accountable to Him for. It is wrong to believe we can get away with sin when there is no true repentance from our hearts. God knows if we are truly repentant or not for He knows our minds and hearts.

A Bible school student surprised me once when he asked if it is okay to keep on having sex with a woman if you repent each time you do it. (He was referring to sex outside of marriage.) I told him that he wasn't really repenting if he didn't want to change his lifestyle. He was not to live under the lie that it was okay to keep on sinning and that God would forgive him each time he sinned. Yes, God forgives us but He also tells us to sin no more. The prostitute knew how much she had been forgiven, for with her tears, she wiped Jesus' feet with her hair. She was a changed woman on the inside and was now to leave her old ways and step into a new lifestyle (Luke 7:36-48).

If we are truly in awe of God and know Him intimately as our Lord and Saviour and Heavenly Father, then we will long to do His will and live in His Presence. There are many blessings we receive from 'fearing the Lord' as we find written in the book of Psalms and Proverbs such as wisdom, knowledge, provision, security, etc. We need to find the balance in our lives of fearing God and having an intimate relationship with Him. They are like opposite sides of the same coin. I believe God is calling His bride back to a lifestyle of holiness. To seek after holiness is to fear the Lord. As we seek His Presence, His Spirit will expose any sin that needs to be dealt with. In His Presence, there is intimacy and holiness. God is calling us to live in His Presence which includes a lifestyle of holiness.

Servant Heart

When I stepped into mission work it came as a surprise when I was first asked to sort out the clinic. Someone needed to go through all the drugs and discard what was out of date or no longer viable. Now to some this wouldn't be a problem, but for me it was a step backwards for I thought I had come to do medical outreaches and not this. But this is exactly what God wanted me first to understand. I had to be willing to serve in ways I wouldn't have personally chosen. Jesus told His disciples that He came not to be served but to serve (Mathew 20:28). In Luke 22, Jesus taught His disciples that the one who is greatest in the Kingdom of God, is the one who serves. Jesus Himself set the example as He demonstrated His servant heart to His disciples when He washed their feet (John 13:1-17).

This was a season where I had to be willing to serve by doing things I didn't want to do before I could serve doing the things that God had put on my heart. At the right timing, after three months of waiting, God released me into the work He had called me to do.

As we fulfil being His faithful servants, He will then call us to be His friends (John 15:15). This doesn't stop us from serving others but our relationship has now become one of friendship where He will reveal Kingdom mysteries and truths. Jesus said that His Father will honour the one who serves Him (John 12:26). We must always be willing to serve our brothers and sisters in Christ, even if we are more experienced than them. God is always looking for those who are willing to serve joyfully and without complaining. Jesus is our servant King who has called us to follow Him and be willing to serve others.

Faith

About ten years ago whilst on a summer holiday, I decided to have fun out on a catamaran in the Mediterranean Sea. As I ventured out with the boatman, the winds started to get up. We were having an exhilarating time as the sail of the boat caught the fast winds and we went at top notch along the ocean. The ride was both exhilarating and scary. I felt we were going to capsize each time the catamaran was half submerged on its side in the sea. Though I was with an experienced yacht's man, he was only a teenager and, funnily enough, a medical student. This didn't stop me from thinking we were going to capsize as we went hurtling along at full speed. When we came back to shore, I thanked him for an amazing ride. I encouraged a friend who was with me to go out and experience it but she fervently said, 'No way!' She was going to stay on the shore where she felt safe and secure and not step into the dangers at sea. She missed out on an amazing experience. It was then that God spoke clearly to me that this is what faith is about. Faith is 'risk' taking! Though it may initially seem daunting as we step out in faith to ride the waves with God, in return we will have such an amazing experience beyond what we can ever dream or imagine.

Many Christians think faith is simply believing in God. Well, the devil believes in God too, so how would that make us any different? Faith is a willingness to step out into the unknown when God asks us to follow Him. It is obeying Him and believing He is with us and will lead us. It is believing He will provide for us and protect us and our families when He has called us to follow and co-labour with Him. Faith is more than hope; it is believing in the unseen.

Faith comes from hearing and hearing comes from the Word of God (Romans 10:17). This can refer to what God is saying through His written Word but actually the Greek word used here is *rhema* which means breathed word or revelation of His Spirit. It is what we see taking place in the Heavenly realm to declare and call it forth here on earth. Faith is knowing God will do what He has promised.

Jesus told His disciples many times, 'Do not fear, have faith!' Faith is greater than our feelings or emotions (especially fear, anxiety or oppression) or our natural understanding on things. There is a saying, 'Fear knocked at the door but faith opened it and no one was there'. It has also been said that 'FEAR' is 'False Evidence Appearing Real'.

One morning as I woke up from my sleep while in Africa, I felt the Presence of God come and rest on me as He said, 'Faith overcomes fear'. I then realised that faith was a response in my spirit, where fear was a response in my soul. My spirit was to rise above my emotions in order for me to step out in faith. I have also come to realise that the enemy will try and throw his stronghold of fear at us for every new thing or new level of work that God is leading us into. We are to realise this and not give into this fear but overcome it with faith! Again Jesus said to His disciples, 'Do not fear, have faith!'

Another time as I was walking on the beach and looking out at the Indian Ocean, I felt the Holy Spirit tell me my time of walking on the shore was now up and I was being called to a radical life of walking on water. It wasn't enough to dip my feet in the water, remain in control and feel safe on the shore. *Was I willing to completely immerse all of myself in Him, so my feet no longer touched the shore?* Instead I was to be dependent on Him for everything and choose to live a life of faith. This meant I had to risk everything I had and all that mattered to me. I saw how we can be toe dippers or paddlers and still have control over our lives, doing what we want. Or we can choose to fully immerse ourselves into His living water and go with the flow of His Spirit, being completely surrendered to His will at all times.

Faith is a choice as we say yes to God and step out into the unknown, totally trusting our lives in His hands. Our security rests in keeping our eyes on Him and holding onto His hand as He leads us the way forth. Faith requires action. Just as the body without the spirit is dead, so faith without deeds is dead (James 2:26). Whenever we struggle with our faith, we can always ask God to give us the gift of faith, which is a gift of the Spirit.

Love and Humility

It's kindness that leads to repentance (Romans 2:4). When people look into your eyes and see the love and compassion of God, then they are more willing to trust what you say and let you pray for them. The Holy Spirit moves through us when we operate in His love, compassion and humility.

Many times in clinic when I came across menial cases I would think, 'What am I doing here?' But then my spirit would say, 'Choose to love even the smallest, insignificant case that comes through the clinic door'. What a challenge this was for me. Life is about sacrificing self for His love. We are to 'do everything in love' (1 Corinthians 16:14).

When we get offended by others it is usually because our pride has been hurt. I used to think being offended was an acceptable thing in life, until I realised being offended by someone meant I hadn't fully dealt with the pride in that area of my life. If we are truly dead to all things of our flesh, then we will not get offended by comments or actions made by man. We need to let go of pride and respect. Jesus never demanded respect. God is no respecter of persons (Romans 2:11). But we are to honour others and honour God, just as God honours us as His children. This is an act of humility and love.

God gave me a vision one time while in Toronto, Canada. In the vision I saw myself going down the Niagara Falls. Waterfalls have spiritually represented two things to me. When I have gone down them they have represented an area in my life that I have had to die to. However, if I have stood under them, they have represented a spiritual blessing and outpouring on my life. After going down the falls, I asked God what I needed to let go of in my life. To my surprise He said, 'Death to reputation and respect'. He said it had to go. I must no longer be concerned about what others think or speak of me.

Jesus didn't care what man thought about Him. He lived a life of meekness and love, never seeking the top position. He never lusted after power, even when Satan tempted Him in the desert. He always did as He saw His Father doing, for He was about His Father's business, not His own. Many whom He healed He did so in secret and told them not to tell others for He didn't want a crowd to come after Him. He didn't care what others spoke about Him. He never sought after attention.

I believe we need to keep the cross central to all we do so we don't get caught up in focusing on our own success or significance. Jesus told His disciples that a tree bearing fruit still needs pruning if it is to bear more fruit (John 15:2). We must be willing to be continually pruned if we want to grow more and bear more fruit in His Kingdom. Pruning may not feel pleasant at the time but we need to go through it if we want to yield a greater harvest for Him.

Grace

Grace is the supernatural ability and power to do what we know we couldn't do in the natural. Jesus is grace personified. I believe there is nothing in our relationship or walk with God that doesn't involve His grace. To understand what grace is, we need understand humility. It was by *grace that we were saved* and not through any works of our own (Ephesians 2:5-7, 2 Timothy 1:9). We can't earn or work for our salvation. It is a free gift by the grace of God. We have different *spiritual gifts according to His grace* given to us. We have done nothing to earn these gifts. They were given through His grace at work in us (Romans 12:6, Ephesians 4:7).

Grace is needed in our lives to live and move under the anointing of the Holy Spirit. Much *grace was upon the apostles* who moved in the *power and anointing* of the Spirit (Acts 4:29-33). Stephen was a man full of *grace and power* as he did many signs and miracles (Acts 6:8). Paul testified much in his letters to the grace of God, for he was called to be an apostle by the grace of God (Romans 1:5). He knew what it was to live under the power of grace. As he cried out to God to remove the spirit of affliction that was on him, God replied, '*My grace is sufficient for you for My power is made perfect in your weakness*' (2 Corinthians 12:9). Paul then proclaimed that when he is weak, then he is strong. Grace gives us strength in our weaknesses. We are not to live under the love of law but the law of love and grace.

It is during the seasons of walking through a time of brokenness in my spirit that I have come to a greater awareness of what grace is truly about. If we are lacking grace, we need to invite God to take us to a place of brokenness and humility with Him.

Teamwork

Most of my mission work has involved working in a team with others. This has been such an important part of character building. God knows which people to put in our teams so we can be sharpened even further. I see that we were created to be a part of the Body of Christ and to inter-depend on one another and work together as part of a family. We all need one another for support and encouragement but also to discipline each other in love, so we can all become Christ-like in our attitudes and lifestyles and prevent one another from stumbling. It is important we recognise each other's talents, gifts and anointing so we can work in harmony and unity with each other.

God has created us to live and work together and not be on our own. We need each other and to recognise each other's God-given abilities so He may flow and dwell in His body, the church. I don't believe single people are to live alone, but to live with other believers where they can have fellowship and grow more in the Spirit. We need to be willing to receive discipline and rebuke, when it is done in love and when it is for our best interest. We need the body of Christ to help us see our weaknesses or spiritual blind spots, hence we need to be accountable to others and let others speak into our lives. Teamwork should be viewed like that of living in a royal family. It is to honour and submit to the one who has the authority and leadership role but to also honour and love each other as brothers and sisters in Christ.

Fasting

Many times we just want to get right in there and reap the harvest but there are times when we need to bring down enemy strongholds first before we can take ground in the Kingdom. This may require prayer and fasting. There are different ways to fast and we need to seek God as to what type and for how long. Some are called to 40-day fasts, others to one-day fasts on a weekly basis. Daniel did a 21-day partial fast when praying for a breakthrough in his nation; whereas Ester did a three day total fast of no food or water in order to save her fellow Jewish people from destruction.

After a season of outreaches, God called me to a two-week fast. He was walking me through what seemed like a refiner's fire. I had such peace and grace that I didn't even have an appetite or miss my food. I just drank fluids and sought more of God in my spirit. It was a key time for God to transform me and further crucify my flesh.

I believe fasting is a way of life for all who want to step into a Kingdom lifestyle for God. It is a spiritual discipline, but needs also to be led by the Holy Spirit. Fasting puts aside all soulish needs and focuses our spirit on God. Our spirit is strengthened during a fast (even if we feel physically weak during a whole fast). Jesus was led by the Holy Spirit to fast for 40 days in the desert. Though He came out of the fast feeling very hungry, He was in the *power* of the Spirit. He was about to fulfil all that was written in the first verses of Isaiah 61 as He entered into His full time ministry (Luke 4:14-20). I believe fasting is a key for spiritual breakthrough in our lives and the lives of others as well as bringing forth God's Kingdom on earth!

Resurrected Life
Without a death in our flesh we cannot enter a resurrected life in the Spirit. As we let God deal with our carnal nature and surrender each area to be crucified on the cross, we will live in greater measure under the power of His Spirit. I believe that as God asks us to surrender the things in our life that matter to us, He will replace our death to self with a resurrected life in Him. We will then go from glory to glory.

I have come to understand that a resurrected life in the Spirit involves a continual laying down of one's life to God instead of trying to be in control of it ourselves. As Paul said, '*I have crucified myself with Christ, for it is no longer I who lives but Christ who lives in me*' (Galatians 2:20).

We cannot enter into a resurrected life in the Spirit unless we are willing to put our carnal life to death first. When Jesus told His disciples to follow Him, He meant they had to pick up their cross and be willing to lay down their lives for Him. Jesus also asks us to do the same thing. This is so we can enter into the fullness of a resurrected life in His Spirit.

Paul said, '*I consider everything a loss compared to the surpassing greatness of knowing Jesus my Lord, for whose sake I have lost all things. I want to know Christ and the power of His resurrection and fellowship of sharing in His sufferings, becoming like Him in His death and somehow attain to the resurrection from the dead*' (Philippians 3:8, 10). In the natural, death is the end of life; but in the supernatural, death to self is the beginning of a resurrected life in the Spirit.

When Jesus appeared to His disciples after He rose from the dead, He said to them, '*Do not leave Jerusalem but wait for the gift My Father promised, which you have heard Me speak about. For John baptized with water but in a few days you will be baptized with the Holy Spirit*'. He continued, '*It is not for you to know the times or dates the Father has set by His own authority.* **But you will receive power when the Holy Spirit comes on you; and you will be My witnesses in Jerusalem and in all Judea and Samaria and to the ends of the earth**' (Acts 1:4-8).

It is amazing that the Greek word for 'power' used in this context is '*dunamis*', where we get the word 'dynamite' from. And according to Strong's Concordance, the Greek word for 'witness' is '*martus*', which also means 'martyr' or witness unto death. Jesus was telling His disciples that they would receive His miraculous power and be martyrs or witnesses who were willing to risk their lives unto death for Him. The disciples had to be willing to lay their lives down for Him in order to be carriers of His *dunamis* power. You can't have one without the other! This is the cost if you want to carry His *dunamis* power. It will come in God's timing and He is looking for those who are so hungering after Him that they are willing to sacrifice their all, even their lives.

Conclusion

Kingdom Medicine is all about healing the sick, binding up the broken hearted, setting the captives free and bringing the lost into God's Kingdom, thus revealing His awesome power and passionate love for each person. It is also about co-labouring with

179

the Great Physician Himself, Jesus. The good news is that this is only for our time on earth, for in Heaven there will be no sickness or disease, no curses or tears or pain. '*And I heard a loud voice from the throne saying, "Now the dwelling of God is with men, and He will live with them. He will wipe every tear from their eyes. There will be no more death or mourning or crying or pain, for the old order of things has passed away"*' (Revelation 21:3-4).

We are in a spiritual battle during our time on earth where the enemy is trying to kill, steal and destroy people's lives. We are called to take our stand in God's Kingdom. We need to realise the spiritual authority that we have as God's children to come against all sickness and disease and not fear any demonic spirit or enemy stronghold.

I pray that as you enter your spiritual calling and destiny, you will see sickness and disease through new lenses. We are called to set the captives free, release the prisoners, bind up the broken hearted, open the eyes of the blind and the ears of the deaf, make the lame run and even raise the dead! This is our mandate, this is our calling. If we all play our part, I believe the sooner Jesus will return.

Appendix A

TESTIMONIES FROM TEAM HELPERS

Here are some testimonies from the various people who came and helped on the different medical outreaches in Africa. For some, English is their second language. We didn't record all the testimonies from each outreach, but here are some that were documented. They have been typed as they were written. Names have been initialed for safety and confidentiality purposes.

June 2007

At noon I asked the Lord to show me His power. I don't want to ask to see just a big healing miracle- I asked the Lord to show me His power in the way He wants to show it to me. In the afternoon, I was praying outside the tent for sick people. I waited one hour for someone to come and translate for me so I could tell a lady about Jesus. A group of people gathered to hear what I was saying to the lady. One man joined in the discussion, quite aggressively. He was against Jesus and fought for the witchdoctor's treatment. After more than one hour, he started to agree with the pastor who was translating. And finally, he was very happy that Jesus was preached to this village- to his village! He was the village chief! He told the woman to cut off the fetishes on her two children and not to go back to the witchdoctor. Then we prayed for the woman and the children to get healed- they sure got healed. We were going to leave but a young man who also attended the whole discussion stopped us. He wanted to receive Jesus. We prayed together and had big joy about this new brother in the family!

I was privileged to go on another medical outreach. I was in front of the tent, triaging the people when a big man showed up. I told him he had to wait in the queue. The local translator heard that he was an official policeman. So we decided to let him sooner into the clinic as he had not much time. Actually, he had come because he heard that there were people coming who were speaking about Jesus- In the tent he was treated and when they prayed for him the Holy Spirit started to pour out visions and prophecies over him. He left a very happy man.

- Anonymous

<u>*July 2007*</u>

I want to thank God for giving me an opportunity to go on this medical outreach. I wasn't sure what to expect but I was very excited after the prayer time we had together. On Saturday I got to intercede outside the medical tent and later prayed for the people. So many were healed of headaches, backaches, etc. There was one old man who touched my heart. He said he had back pain which ran down his leg. So me and a few others prayed for him. At the end I felt God wanted him to jump. I asked him and he did and he bent and stretched. He was healed indeed and he had a beautiful smile on his face. God was healing His people and it was amazing to see them totally free!

One of the mum's was holding her beautiful little baby and she wanted prayer. As I started praying I noticed the witchcraft thread (fetish) around her neck and ankle. After we explained things, she found a knife and cut those threads. I prayed for her and the baby and the little one started to smile with me so much and made such beautiful baby noises as if to say something. I will never forget that little baby's face and beautiful smile.

On Sunday, we put up the tent and prayed again but we were all tired. As always, God broke through. There were 5 old women who came to the tent and all of them left the tent accepting Jesus, being healed and not needing any medication. I was so touched by His goodness and love for His people. I know He doesn't need us for anything, but He has given us His awesome privilege of carrying His Spirit, His love, His healing grace to all people.

It was truly one of the best weekends I've had during the Holy Given School.

- N.J.

<u>*August 2007*</u>

In the short time we had doing medical, it was an amazing experience! God's Glory fell in the tent & many were set free from sickness, witchcraft & curses. It was amazing to see how God used us as a team to break down strongholds one by one- bringing Heaven to earth, one person at a time. God has truly blessed this strategy- truly a Kingdom work!

God really opened my eyes & healed my heart in places by watching Him move among the poorest of the poor & heal the sick & set the captives free! I was honored to have been a part of this amazing Kingdom work! Thank you Jesus! Oh by the way, a woman who had sexual relations with a witchdoctor & made a blood covenant with him, was completely set free & gave her heart to the Lord! Amen!

    - Anonymous

August 2007

I helped one day to de-worm and pray over the children. As we laid hands on each child, proclaiming life and health over each one in the name of Jesus and praying into their identities and callings and destinies, the Lord gave me a picture. This picture communicated to me His vision for how important it is to pray over the children. I saw each child walk away covered with the Presence of God and then walking around their villages as little light bubbles, protected and advancing the kingdom. The more children prayed for and dedicated to Jesus, the more darkness had to flee. Through this, the Lord emphasized to me how important and powerful it is to pray for and lay hands on the children. The de-worming is just an excuse to claim and cover these children for the Kingdom.

    - S

August 2007 -Extended outreach

Whilst praying for a mother & her baby, I felt the Lord saying the family was trapped under the curse of witchcraft and especially fear. The baby was crying uncontrollably and refused to take the de-worming medication. We prayed & broke the curse in Jesus' Name & then almost immediately, the baby stopped crying & his face was transformed. The baby's and mother's countenance completely changed and they began smiling. Praise Jesus for His goodness!

    - A

October 2007

As I was praying for a little boy, about 6 years old, God told me he was going to be a pastor. Later that morning, a man came to me and asked if I could pray for him and his knee. I was still with the little boy who had a strange, unstable breathing (and was waiting for the doctor). I laid the boy's hands on this man's knee and the boy repeated after me, 'Jesus Christ, Heal!' I don't know what happened to the man but the boy was healed!

    - Anonymous

October 2007

A thin old lady came into the tent and sat down with Dr Angie and several on the team. She denied having been to a witchdoctor (undoubtedly she had), so Angie asked her if she believed Jesus could heal her. She answered, 'How could I believe He could heal me if I don't even know who He is?' Angie proceeded to tell her who He is, lovingly translated by Peter, whose heart seemed involved in the translation. She accepted Jesus. She had previously complained of sickness in her head, heart and stomach. When we first prayed, she said her headache was gone but the rest remained. We prayed (with translation) for God's love to be revealed to her. Some of the words about her hard life and depression, touched her, and tears fell down her face. Her stomach pain was gone. She was elated. She playfully danced briefly and said she would never believe in any other power than Jesus.

    - K.O.

November 2007

I was in one of the queues giving out the de-worming tablets to the children. We had half a bottle of water and started giving out the tablets. I noticed that the bottle of tablets was emptying quickly and that there was only a few tablets left, but after prayer, we carried on giving out the tablets with the water. Many, many more children kept arriving for the treatment and finally we finished. When we looked at the bottle of water we realized that it hadn't run out and there was the same amount of tablets left, even though we'd given out loads more tablets to more children!

    - B & H

December 2008

I have been given a 'continuing medical education' course with Dr Angie. I've had a whole paradigm shift from looking at the spiritual as an adjunctive to seeing it as a primary. And then I watched God demonstrate this time and time again. My world has been rocked!

    - K.G.

Appendix B

REFERENCES

CHAPTER ONE

1. Chambers, Oswald. *My Utmost for His Highest*, (Discovery House Publishers, 2012), August 30.
2. Lockley, Tom (2005). *See His Love*. Thankyou Music.

CHAPTER TWO

1. For more information go to www.irisglobal.org.

CHAPTER EIGHT

1. Johnson, Bill. *When Heaven Invades Earth*, (Destiny Image Publishers, 2007), p 113.
2. Pierce, Cal. *Preparing the Way: The Reopening of the John G. Lake Healing Rooms in Spokane, Washington*, (McDougal Publishing Company, 2001), Chapter 5.
3. Kenneth Copeland Publishing. *John G Lake, A Strong Man's Gospel*, p XXI.

CHAPTER TEN

1. Liardon, Roberts. *Smith Wigglesworth on Prayer, Power, and Miracles*, (Destiny Image Publishers, 2005), p 204-207.

CHAPTER TWELVE

1. Liardon, Robert. *John G Lake: Complete Collection of His Teaching,* (Whitaker House, 2005), pp 12, 335, 367, 372.
2. Lake, John G. and Kenneth Copeland. *John G Lake: His Life, His Sermons, His Boldness of Faith,* (Harrison House Publishers, 2013), p 483.
3. Lake, John G. and Kenneth Copeland. *John G Lake: His Life, His Sermons, His Boldness of Faith,* (Harrison House Publishers, 2013), p xxi.

Appendix C

ABOUT THE AUTHOR

Angela trained at Liverpool Medical School where she qualified as a doctor in 1991. Two years later, she decided to further her career in paediatrics and trained in the London teaching hospitals. After becoming a Member of the Royal College of Paediatrics & Child Health (RCPCH), she obtained a Master's Degree in Clinical Paediatrics at Great Ormond Street Hospital, London. Shortly after, she took a Diploma in Tropical Medicine and Hygiene at Liverpool School of Tropical Medicine. After this she worked for eighteen months as a paediatric lecturer with Voluntary Services Oversees (VSO) on the RCPCH/VSO 'registrar training scheme' in Uganda. In 2004 she completed her specialist registrar training in London and became a consultant in paediatrics and child health. A year later she studied for a year at a Mission Bible College (All Nations Christian College in Hertfordshire). Shortly after, she joined Iris Global in 2006 where she served as a medical missionary. During her time in Africa, she has taught and ministered in the churches, in Bible Schools, in local hospitals and in the local prisons, as well as tending the needs of the children on the Iris bases.

For further enquiries email: kingdomedicine@gmail.com

Made in the USA
Charleston, SC
26 November 2014